READING SKILLS

LEARNINGEXPRESS BASIC SKILLS FOR COLLEGE

READING SKILLS

FOR COLLEGE STUDENTS

Elizabeth Chesla

Prentice Hall

Library of Congress Cataloging-in-Publication Data

Chesla, Elizabeth L.
    Reading skills for college students / Elizabeth L. Chesla
        p.   cm.—(LearningExpress basic skills for college)
    ISBN 0–13–080258–1
    1. Reading(Higher education) 2. College readers. 3.Reading
    comprehension.   I. Title. II. Series.
LB2395.3.C54   1998   97–43621
428.4'071'1—dc21   CIP

Acquisitions Editor: *Todd Rossell*
Managing Editor: *Mary Carnis*
Director of Manufacturing & Production: *Bruce Johnson*
Manufacturing Buyer: *Marc Bove*
Editorial Assistant: *Amy Diehl*

© 1998 by LearningExpress, LLC.
Published by Prentice Hall, Inc.
Simon & Schuster/A Viacom Company
Upper Saddle River, New Jersey 07458

Printed in the United States of America
10   9   8   7   6   5   4   3   2   1

ISBN: 0–13–080258–1

Prentice Hall International (UK) Limited, *London*
Prentice Hall of Australia Pty. Limited, *Sydney*
Prentice Hall of Canada Inc., *Toronto*
Prentice Hall Hispanoamericana, S.A., *Mexico*
Prentice Hall of India Private Limited, *New Delhi*
Prentice Hall of Japan, Inc., *Tokyo*
Simon & Schuster Asia Pte. Ltd., *Singapore*
Editora Prentice Hall do Brasil, Ltda., *Rio de Janeiro*

OTHER TITLES FROM PRENTICE HALL

ACKNOWLEDGEMENTS

We would like to thank the following people for reviewing the Basic Skills for College series. These books are better as a result of their time and effort:

Jerry Bouchie, St. Cloud State University

Kathy Carpenter, Ph.D., University of Nebraska at Kearney

Dr. Thomas R. Gier, University of Alaska, Anchorage

Karen R. Olson, University of New Mexico

Celesia Snyder, Ohio State University, Newark/Central Ohio Technical College

Very special thanks for their efforts go to Jan Gallagher, James Gish, and Barry Lippman at LearningExpress. Their efforts and those of their staff were essential and invaluable in making this series successful.

We appreciate the hours of diligent work of those at Prentice Hall: Mary Carnis, Marc Bove, Santos Shih, Rit Dojny, Irene Hess, Dave Jagger, Julio Cassanelli, Bryon Smith, Clarence Diehl, Sue Bierman, Juanita Griffin, Katie Bradford, Frank Mortimer, Christopher Eastman, Todd Rossell, and especially to Amy Diehl for her tireless hours of service.

LearningExpress Basic Skills for College

Build basic skills *fast!* Each book offers essential tips and techniques plus plenty of practice exercises in critical skill areas. Ideal for beginning college students who need to brush up on the basics. A must for those who need to polish the skills that lead to success.

Math Skills for College Students (ISBN 0-13-080257-3)
Reading Skills for College Students (ISBN 0-13-080258-1)
Vocabulary & Spelling Skills for College Students (ISBN 0-13-080255-7)
Writing Skills for College Students (ISBN 0-13-080256-5)

CONTENTS

Language and Style

Reading Between the Lines

INTRODUCTION

As a college student, you'll spend many hours in the classroom, listening to lectures and participating in discussions. But much of your academic learning will take place outside the classroom—when you're alone with your books. Whether you major in English or economics, chemistry or computer science, most of the material you'll need to master will come from books. You will be expected not only to understand what you read but also to be able to respond to and assess what you read. That's why strong reading comprehension and critical thinking skills are so essential for college success.

HOW TO USE THIS BOOK

This book will help you build those critical reading and thinking skills in lessons that only take a short amount of time each day to complete. You'll start with the basics and move into more complex reading comprehension and critical thinking strategies. Please note that although each chapter can be an effective skill builder on its own, it is important that you proceed through this book in order, from Lesson 1 through Lesson 23. Each lesson builds on skills and ideas discussed in the previous chapters. As you move through this book and your reading skills develop, the passages you read will increase both in length and in complexity.

The text is divided into four sections, each focusing on a different group of related reading and thinking strategies. These strategies will be outlined at the beginning of each section and then reviewed in a special "putting it all together" final lesson.

Each lesson provides several exercises that allow you to practice the skills you learn. To help you be sure you're on the right track, each lesson also provides answers and explanations for all of the practice questions. You will also find practical suggestions in each chapter for how to continue practicing these skills throughout the rest of the day and the week.

The most important thing you need to know in order to successfully read your college textbooks is how to be an active reader. Really, this whole book is about becoming an active reader. But the rest of this introduction will tell you a few of the most important points about active reading, so you can start practicing them right away in Lesson 1.

BECOMING AN ACTIVE READER

Critical reading and thinking skills require active reading. Being an active reader means you have to engage yourself with the text, both mentally and physically. Active readers generally do this in three ways:

- By skimming ahead and jumping back
- By marking up the text
- By making specific observations about the text

SKIMMING AHEAD AND JUMPING BACK

Skimming ahead enables you to see what's coming up in your reading. Page through the text you're about to read. Notice how the text is broken down, what the main topics are, and the order in which they are covered. Notice key words and ideas that are boldfaced, bulleted, boxed, or otherwise highlighted. By skimming through

the text like this beforehand, you prepare yourself for your reading task. It's a lot like checking out the hills and curves in the course before a cross-country race. If you know what's ahead, you know how to pace yourself, and you're prepared to handle what's to come.

When you finish your reading task, jump back. Review the summaries, headings, and highlighted information in the text. Include both what the author highlighted and what you highlighted. By jumping back, you help to solidify in your mind the ideas and information you just read. You're reminded of how each idea fits into the whole, how ideas and information are connected. When you make connections between ideas, you're much more likely to remember them.

MARKING UP THE TEXT

Marking up the text creates a direct physical link between you and the words you're reading. It forces you to pay closer attention to the words that you read and takes you to a higher level of comprehension. Marking up the text includes three specific strategies:

- Highlighting or underlining key words and ideas
- Circling and defining any unfamiliar words or phrases
- Recording your reactions and questions in the margins

Highlighting or Underlining Key Ideas

When you highlight or underline key words and ideas, you mark the most important parts of the text you are reading. There's an important skill at work here: You can't highlight or underline everything, so you have to distinguish between the facts and ideas that are most important (major ideas) and those facts and ideas that are helpful but not so important (minor or supporting ideas). You want to highlight only the major ideas, so you don't end up with a text that's completely highlighted.

When your text is highlighted, you'll benefit much more from a review of the text—when you jump back, you'll be quickly reminded of the most important ideas to remember. Having highlighted or underlined major ideas also helps you study efficiently for a midterm or final exam.

Circling Unfamiliar Words

One of the most important habits to develop is that of circling and looking up unfamiliar words and phrases. If possible, don't sit down to read without a dictionary by your side. It is not uncommon for the meaning of an entire sentence to hinge on the meaning of a single word or phrase, and if you don't know what that word or phrase means, you won't understand the sentence. Besides, this habit enables you to quickly and steadily expand your vocabulary, and you'll be a more confident reader and speaker as a result.

If you don't have a dictionary readily available, try to determine the meaning of the word as best you can from its context—that is, the words and ideas around it. (There's more on this topic in Lesson 3.) Then, make sure you look up the word as soon as possible so you're sure what it means.

Making Marginal Notes

Recording your questions and reactions in the margins turns you from a passive receiver of information into an active participant in a dialogue. (If you're reading a library book, write your reactions in a notebook.) You will get much more out of the ideas and information you read about if you create a "conversation" with the writer. Here are some examples of the kinds of reactions you might write down in the margin or in your notebook:

- **Questions** often come up when you read. They may be answered later in the text or by your instructor, but by that time you may have forgotten the question! And if your question isn't answered, you may want to bring it up in class: "Why does the writer describe the new welfare policy as 'unfair'?" or "Why does the character react in this way?"
- **Agreements and disagreements** with the author are bound to come up if you're reading actively. Write them down: "That's not necessarily true!" or "This policy makes a lot of sense to me."
- **Connections** you note can be either between the text and something that you read earlier or between the text and your own experience. For example, "I remember feeling the same way when I . . . ." or "This is similar to what happened in China."
- **Evaluations** are your way of keeping the author honest. If you think the author isn't providing sufficient support for what he or she is saying, or that there's something wrong with that support, say so: "He says the dropping of the bomb was inevitable, but he doesn't explain why" or "This is a very selfish reason."

MAKING OBSERVATIONS

Good readers know that writers use many different strategies to express their ideas. Even if you know very little about those strategies, you can make useful observations about what you read that will help you better understand and remember the author's ideas. You can notice, for example, the author's choice of words; the structure of the sentences and paragraphs; any repetition of words or ideas; important details about people, places, and things; and so on.

This step—making observations—is essential because your observations, what you notice, are what lead you to logical inferences about what you read. *Inferences* are conclusions based on reason, fact, or evidence. You are constantly making inferences based on your observations, even when you're not reading. For example, if you notice that the sky is full of dark, heavy clouds, you might infer that it is going to rain; if you notice that your roommate has a stack of library books on her desk, you might infer that she is working on a research paper.

If you misunderstand what you read, it is often because you haven't looked closely enough at the text. As a result, you base your inferences on your own ideas and experiences, not on what's actually written in the text. You end up forcing your own ideas on the author rather than listening to what the author has to say and then forming your own ideas about it. It's critical, then, that you begin to really pay attention to what writers say and how they say it.

If any of this sounds a bit confusing now, don't worry. Each of these ideas will be explained thoroughly in the lessons that follow. What's important in the meantime is that you start practicing active reading as best you can. Begin by skimming ahead and marking up the text in Lesson 1.

PRETEST

Before you start your study of reading skills, you may want to get an idea of how much you already know and how much you need to learn. If that's the case, take the pretest that follows. The pretest is 50 multiple-choice questions covering all the lessons in this book. Naturally, 50 questions can't cover every single concept or strategy you will learn by working through this book. So even if you get all of the questions on the pretest right, it's almost guaranteed that you will find a few ideas or reading tactics in this book that you didn't already know. On the other hand, if you get a lot of the answers wrong on this pretest, don't despair. This book will show you how to read more effectively, step by step.

So use this pretest just to get a general idea of how much of what's in this book you already know. If you get a high score on this pretest, you may be able to spend less time with this book than you originally planned. If you get a low score, you may find that you will need more than 20 minutes a day to get through each chapter and improve your reading skills.

There's an answer sheet you can use for filling in the correct answers on the next page. Or, if you prefer, simply circle the answer numbers in this book. If the book doesn't belong to you, write the numbers 1–50 on a piece of paper and record your answers there. Take as much time as you need to do this short test. When you finish, check your answers against the answer key at the end of this lesson. Each answer tells you which lesson of this book teaches you about the reading strategy in that question.

1.	ⓐ	ⓑ	ⓒ	ⓓ
2.	ⓐ	ⓑ	ⓒ	ⓓ
3.	ⓐ	ⓑ	ⓒ	ⓓ
4.	ⓐ	ⓑ	ⓒ	ⓓ
5.	ⓐ	ⓑ	ⓒ	ⓓ
6.	ⓐ	ⓑ	ⓒ	ⓓ
7.	ⓐ	ⓑ	ⓒ	ⓓ
8.	ⓐ	ⓑ	ⓒ	ⓓ
9.	ⓐ	ⓑ	ⓒ	ⓓ
10.	ⓐ	ⓑ	ⓒ	ⓓ
11.	ⓐ	ⓑ	ⓒ	ⓓ
12.	ⓐ	ⓑ	ⓒ	ⓓ
13.	ⓐ	ⓑ	ⓒ	ⓓ
14.	ⓐ	ⓑ	ⓒ	ⓓ
15.	ⓐ	ⓑ	ⓒ	ⓓ
16.	ⓐ	ⓑ	ⓒ	ⓓ
17.	ⓐ	ⓑ	ⓒ	ⓓ
18.	ⓐ	ⓑ	ⓒ	ⓓ
19.	ⓐ	ⓑ	ⓒ	ⓓ
20.	ⓐ	ⓑ	ⓒ	ⓓ
21.	ⓐ	ⓑ	ⓒ	ⓓ
22.	ⓐ	ⓑ	ⓒ	ⓓ
23.	ⓐ	ⓑ	ⓒ	ⓓ
24.	ⓐ	ⓑ	ⓒ	ⓓ
25.	ⓐ	ⓑ	ⓒ	ⓓ
26.	ⓐ	ⓑ	ⓒ	ⓓ
27.	ⓐ	ⓑ	ⓒ	ⓓ
28.	ⓐ	ⓑ	ⓒ	ⓓ
29.	ⓐ	ⓑ	ⓒ	ⓓ
30.	ⓐ	ⓑ	ⓒ	ⓓ
31.	ⓐ	ⓑ	ⓒ	ⓓ
32.	ⓐ	ⓑ	ⓒ	ⓓ
33.	ⓐ	ⓑ	ⓒ	ⓓ
34.	ⓐ	ⓑ	ⓒ	ⓓ
35.	ⓐ	ⓑ	ⓒ	ⓓ
36.	ⓐ	ⓑ	ⓒ	ⓓ
37.	ⓐ	ⓑ	ⓒ	ⓓ
38.	ⓐ	ⓑ	ⓒ	ⓓ
39.	ⓐ	ⓑ	ⓒ	ⓓ
40.	ⓐ	ⓑ	ⓒ	ⓓ
41.	ⓐ	ⓑ	ⓒ	ⓓ
42.	ⓐ	ⓑ	ⓒ	ⓓ
43.	ⓐ	ⓑ	ⓒ	ⓓ
44.	ⓐ	ⓑ	ⓒ	ⓓ
45.	ⓐ	ⓑ	ⓒ	ⓓ
46.	ⓐ	ⓑ	ⓒ	ⓓ
47.	ⓐ	ⓑ	ⓒ	ⓓ
48.	ⓐ	ⓑ	ⓒ	ⓓ
49.	ⓐ	ⓑ	ⓒ	ⓓ
50.	ⓐ	ⓑ	ⓒ	ⓓ

PRETEST

The pretest consists of a series of reading passages with questions that follow to test your comprehension.

Mt. Kindred Adds Psychology Courses

Mount Kindred College hopes to draw more students from the community with two new early childhood course offerings this fall. Department Chair Jane Fairbanks announced Tuesday that the course titles will be The Myth of the Difficult Child and Three R's or Two T's?: Real Learning or Tantrums in Tandem? The latter course will be an observational lab held at The Learning Academy, the preschool on campus.

New faculty member Dr. Allison Landers will instruct both courses. Landers received her Ph.D. in 1995 from Northwestern University, where she wrote a dissertation on the pedagogical effectiveness of preschools. According to Fairbanks, Dr. Landers concluded that academic results are questionable, but that preschools have extensive side benefits.

The courses are part of Mount Kindred's Project Outreach, which aims to draw more non-traditional students to the college. The project was initiated in 1993, according to Dr. Fairbanks, in order to better serve the five-county area. Mount Kindred is the only college in the region, and the governor-appointed Board of Trustees mandated that more efforts be made to involve the community in college programs. Dr. Fairbanks also disclosed that the college's enrollment has fallen ten percent over the past five years, while the state university in Unionville has seen an increase in enrollment.

The observational course meets one of the Psychology bachelor program lab requirements. It may also be of special interest to parents who wish a greater understanding of childhood learning behaviors. The Myth of the Difficult Child is scheduled on weekday evenings in order to make it easier for working parents to attend. Contact the Psychology Department at 777-4531 for more information, or drop by the office in Powell Hall. Other college departments will be announcing Project Outreach courses in the coming weeks. For a complete listing, refer to the fall course catalogue, available at the Crabtree, the campus bookstore, beginning August 1.

1. The Myth of the Difficult Child course will be held
   a. in Unionville, in order to attract students attending the university there
   b. at the campus pre-school, to allow direct observation of learning environments
   c. at night, for the convenience of people who work during the daytime
   d. in the early morning, so working parents can trade off child-care responsibilities

2. Which of the following statements is correct?
   a. Professor Landers will teach both courses.
   b. People wanting course catalogues should call the Psychology Department.
   c. The new courses begin August 1.
   d. The campus pre-school is called the Crabtree.

3. According to Jane Fairbanks, what was the direct cause of Project Outreach?

   a. The Psychology faculty believed that members of the community should develop a greater understanding of their children's education.

   b. Professor Lander's talents and interests were particularly suited to community involvement.

   c. The Board of Trustees was appointed by the governor in 1993 and needed to find ways to spend its budget.

   d. The Board of Trustees directed Mount Kindred College to strengthen its community involvement efforts.

4. Which of the following factors is implied as another reason for Project Outreach?

   a. Enrollment has been going down, and the college wishes to attract more students.

   b. The college has discriminated against lower-income community members in the past.

   c. Many parents who have previously studied psychology live in the five-county area.

   d. The Board of Trustees wants a more academically vigorous curriculum.

5. From the context of the passage, it can be determined that the word "pedagogical" in Professor Lander's dissertation is related to

   a. unfair attitudes

   b. teaching

   c. psychological disorders

   d. behavior

6. The "Myth of the Difficult Child" course title implies that Professor Landers

   a. believes that telling stories about children will help us understand them better

   b. wants to convince her students of the need for strong behavior controls

   c. questions the validity of the label "difficult" when applied to children

   d. thinks poorly behaved children tell stories in order to justify their behavior

7. Which of the following correctly states the primary subject of this news article?

   a. the politics guiding the decision of the Board of Trustees that led to the establishment of Project Outreach

   b. Professor Lander's appointment to Mount Kindred College's Psychology Department

   c. two new early childhood psychology course offerings at Mount Kindred College

   d. the needs of the community in relation to Mount Kindred College

8. This article is organized in which of the following ways?

   a. in chronological order, from the past to the future

   b. most important information first, followed by background and details

   c. background first, followed by the most important information and details

   d. as sensational news, with the most controversial topic first

(excerpt from the opening of an untitled essay)

John Steinbeck's *Grapes of Wrath*, published in 1939, was followed ten years later by A. B. Guthrie's *The Way West*. Both books chronicle a migration, though that of Guthrie's pioneers is considerably less bleak in origin. What strikes one at first glance, however, are the commonalties. Both Steinbeck's and Guthrie's characters are primarily farmers. They look to their destinations with nearly religious enthusiasm, imagining their "promised" land the way the Biblical Israelites envisioned Canaan. Both undergo great hardship to make the trek. But the two sagas differ distinctly in origin. Steinbeck's Oklahomans are forced off their land by the banks who own their mortgages, and they follow a false promise—that jobs await them as seasonal laborers in California. Guthrie's farmers willingly remove themselves, selling their land and trading their old dreams for their new hope in Oregon. The pioneers' decision to leave their farms in Missouri and the East is frivolous and ill-founded in comparison with the Oklahomans' unwilling response to displacement. Yet it is they, the pioneers, whom our history books declare the heroes.

9. From the context of the passage, it can be determined that the word "frivolous" most nearly means
   a. silly
   b. high-minded
   c. difficult
   d. calculated

10. Suppose that the author is considering following this sentence with supportive detail: "Both undergo great hardship to make the trek." Which of the following sentences would be in keeping with the comparison and contrast structure of the paragraph?
    a. The migrants in *The Way West* cross the Missouri, then the Kaw, and make their way overland to the Platte.
    b. The Oklahomans' jalopies break down repeatedly, while the pioneers' wagons need frequent repairs.
    c. Today's travelers would consider it a hardship to spend several days, let alone several months, getting anywhere.
    d. The Joad family, in *The Grapes of Wrath*, loses both grandmother and grandfather before the journey is complete.

11. Which of the following excerpts from the essay is an opinion, rather than a fact?
    a. "Both Steinbeck's and Guthrie's characters are primarily farmers."
    b. "Steinbeck's Oklahomans are forced off their land by the banks who own their mortgages…."
    c. "John Steinbeck's *Grapes of Wrath*, published in 1939, was followed ten years later by A. B. Guthrie's *The Way West*."
    d. "The pioneers' decision to leave their farms in Missouri and the East is frivolous and ill-founded in comparison with the Oklahomans'…."

12. The language in the paragraph implies that which of the following will happen to the Oklahomans when they arrive in California?
    a. They will find a means to practice their religion freely.
    b. They will be declared national heroes.
    c. They will not find the jobs they hoped for.
    d. They will make their livings as mechanics rather than as farm laborers.

Bill Clinton's Inaugural Address
(excerpt from the opening)

When George Washington first took the oath I have just sworn to uphold, news traveled slowly across the land by horseback, and across the ocean by boat. Now the sights and sounds of this ceremony are broadcast instantaneously to billions around the world. Communications and commerce are global. Investment is mobile. Technology is almost magical, and ambition for a better life is now universal.

We earn our livelihood in America today in peaceful competition with people all across the Earth. Profound and powerful forces are shaking and remaking our world, and the urgent question of our time is whether we can make change our friend and not our enemy. This new world has already enriched the lives of millions of Americans who are able to compete and win in it. But when most people are working harder for less; when others cannot work at all; when the cost of health care devastates families and threatens to bankrupt our enterprises, great and small; when the fear of crime robs law-abiding citizens of their freedom; and when millions of poor children cannot even imagine the lives we are calling them to lead, we have not made change our friend.

13. What is the central topic of the speech so far?
  a. how Americans can keep up with global competition
  b. ways in which technology has undermined our economy
  c. ways in which technology has improved our lives
  d. how change has affected America and our need to adapt

14. By comparing our times with those of George Washington, Bill Clinton demonstrates
  a. how apparently different, but actually similar, the two eras are
  b. how drastically technology has speeded up communications
  c. that presidential inaugurations receive huge media attention
  d. that television is a much more convincing communications tool than print

15. When President Clinton says that "most people are working harder for less," he is
  a. reaching a reasonable conclusion based on evidence he has provided

  b. reaching an unreasonable conclusion based on evidence he has provided
  c. making a generalization that would require evidence before it could be confirmed
  d. making a generalization that is so obvious that evidence is not needed

16. Assuming that Clinton wants to add something about crime being a more serious threat in our time than in George Washington's, which of the following sentences would be most consistent with the tone of the presidential speech?
  a. If I'd been alive in George's day, I would have enjoyed knowing that my wife and child could walk city streets without being mugged.
  b. In George Washington's time, Americans may not have enjoyed as many luxuries, but they could rest in the awareness that their neighborhoods were safe.
  c. George could at least count on one thing. He knew that his family was safe from crime.
  d. A statistical analysis of the overall growth in crime rates since 1789 would reveal that a significant increase has taken place.

The Crossing
Chapter I: The Blue Wall
(excerpt from the opening of a novel by Winston Churchill)

I was born under the Blue Ridge, and under that side which is blue in the evening light, in a wild land of game and forest and rushing waters. There, on the borders of a creek that runs into the Yadkin River, in a cabin that was chinked with red mud, I came into the world a subject of King George the Third, in that part of his realm known as the province of North Carolina.

The cabin reeked of corn-pone and bacon, and the odor of pelts. It had two shakedowns, on one of which I slept under a bearskin. A rough stone chimney was reared outside, and the fireplace was as long as my father was tall. There was a crane in it, and a bake kettle; and over it great buckhorns held my father's rifle when it was not in use. On other horns hung jerked bear's meat and venison hams, and gourds for drinking cups, and bags of seed, and my father's best hunting shirt; also, in a neglected corner, several articles of woman's attire from pegs. These once belonged to my mother. Among them was a gown of silk, of a fine, faded pattern, over which I was wont to speculate. The women at the Cross-Roads, twelve miles away, were dressed in coarse butternut wool and huge sunbonnets. But when I questioned my father on these matters he would give me no answers.

My father was—how shall I say what he was? To this day I can only surmise many things of him. He was a Scotchman born, and I know now that he had a slight Scotch accent. At the time of which I write, my early childhood, he was a frontiersman and hunter. I can see him now, with his hunting shirt and leggins and moccasins; his powder horn, engraved with wondrous scenes; his bullet pouch and tomahawk and hunting knife. He was a tall, lean man with a strange, sad face. And he talked little save when he drank too many "horns," as they were called in that country. These lapses of my father's were a perpetual source of wonder to me—and, I must say, of delight. They occurred only when a passing traveler who hit his fancy chanced that way, or, what was almost as rare, a neighbor. Many a winter night I have lain awake under the skins, listening to a flow of language that held me spellbound, though I understood scarce a word of it.

> "Virtuous and vicious every man must be,
> Few in the extreme, but all in a degree."

The chance neighbor or traveler was no less struck with wonder. And many the time have I heard the query, at the Cross-Roads and elsewhere, "Whar Alec Trimble got his larnin'?"

17. Why did the narrator enjoy it when his father drank too many "horns," or drafts of liquor?
    a. The father spoke brilliantly at those times.
    b. The boy was then allowed to do as he pleased.
    c. These were the only times when the father was not abusive.
    d. The boy was allowed to sample the drink himself.

18. Judging by the sentences surrounding it, the word "surmise" in the third paragraph most nearly means
    a. to form a negative opinion
    b. to praise
    c. to desire
    d. to guess

19. The mention of the dress in the second paragraph is most likely meant to
    a. show the similarity between its owner and other members of the community
    b. show how warm the climate was
    c. show the dissimilarity between its owner and other members of the community
    d. give us insight into the way most of the women of the region dressed

20. It can be inferred from the passage that Alec Trimble is
    a. a traveler
    b. a neighbor
    c. the narrator's father
    d. a poet

21. What is the meaning of the lines of verse quoted in the passage?
    a. Men who pretend to be virtuous are actually vicious.
    b. Moderate amounts of virtuousness and viciousness are present in all men.
    c. Virtuous men cannot also be vicious.
    d. Whether men are virtuous or vicious depends on the difficulty of their circumstances.

22. Which of the following adjectives best describes the region in which the cabin is located?
    a. remote
    b. urban
    c. agricultural
    d. flat

23. The author most likely uses dialect when quoting the question "Whar Alec Trimble got his larnin'?" in order to
    a. show disapproval of the father's drinking
    b. show how people talked down to the narrator
    c. show the speakers' lack of education
    d. mimic the way the father talked

(excerpt from a letter to a pet sitter)

Dear Lee,

   As I told you, I'll be gone until Wednesday morning. Thank you so much for taking on my "children" while I'm away. Like real children, they can be kind of irritating sometimes, but I'm going to enjoy myself so much more knowing they're getting some kind human attention. Remember that Regina (the "queen" in Latin, and she acts like one) is teething. If you don't watch her, she'll chew anything, including her sister, the cat. There are plenty of chew toys around the house. Whenever she starts gnawing on anything illegal, just divert her with one of those. She generally settles right down to a good hour-long chew. Then you'll see her wandering around whimpering with the remains of the toy in her mouth. She gets really frustrated because what she wants is to bury the thing. She'll try to dig a hole between the cushions of the couch. Finding that unsatisfactory, she'll wander some more, discontent, until you solve her problem for her. I usually show her the laundry basket, moving a few clothes so she can bury her toy beneath them. I do sound like a parent, don't I? You have to understand, my own son is practically grown up.

   Regina's food is the Puppy Chow in the utility room, where the other pet food is kept. Give her a bowl once in the morning and once in the evening. No more than that, no matter how much she begs. Beagles are notorious over-eaters, according to her breeder, and I don't want her to lose her girlish figure. She can share Rex (the King's) water, but be sure it's changed daily. She needs to go out several times a day, especially last thing at night and first thing in the morning. Let her stay out for about ten minutes each time, so she can do *all* her business. She also needs a walk in the afternoon, after which it's important to romp with her for awhile in the yard. The game she loves most is fetch, but be sure to make her drop the ball. She'd rather play tug of war with it. Tell her, "Sit!" Then when she does, say, "Drop it!" Be sure to tell her "good girl," and then throw the ball for her. I hope you'll enjoy these sessions as much as I do.

   Now, for the other two, Rex and Paws… (*letter continues*)

24. The tone of this letter is best described as
a. chatty and humorous
b. logical and precise
c. confident and trusting
d. condescending and preachy

25. If the pet sitter is a business-like professional who watches people's pets for a living, she or he would likely prefer
a. more first-person revelations about the owner
b. fewer first-person revelations about the owner
c. more praise for agreeing to watch the animals
d. greater detail on the animals' cute behavior

26. According to the author, his or her attachment to the pets derives at least partially from
a. their regal pedigrees and royal bearing
b. having few friends to pass the time with
c. these particular animals' exceptional needs
d. a desire to continue parenting

27. The information in the note is sufficient to determine that there are three animals. They are
a. two cats and a dog
b. three dogs
c. a dog, a cat, and an unspecified animal
d. a cat, a dog, and a parrot

28. Given that there are three animals to feed, which of the following arrangements of the feeding instructions would be most efficient and easiest to follow?
   a. all given in one list, chronologically from morning to night
   b. provided separately as they are for Regina, within separate passages on each animal
   c. given in the order of quantities needed, the most to the least.
   d. placed in the middle of the letter, where they would be least likely to be overlooked.

29. From the context of the note, it is most likely that the name "Rex" comes from the
   a. Spanish language
   b. English language
   c. French language
   d. Latin language

30. If the sitter is to follow the owner's directions in playing fetch with Regina, at what point will he or she will tell Regina "good girl"?
   a. every time Regina goes after the ball
   b. after Regina finds the ball
   c. when Regina brings the ball back
   d. after Regina drops the ball.

(excerpt from an anti-hunting essay)

The practice of hunting is barbaric and shouldn't be allowed within the national forests of the United States. These forests should be sanctuaries for wildlife, not shooting galleries where macho types go to vent their urban frustrations. Just like humans, animals have the right to freedom and the pursuit of happiness in their own homeland. Of all the forms of hunting, trophy hunting is the most unforgivable. Imagine if it were the other way around and animals were hunting humans. Would it be fair for your grandfather to be killed because of his age and stature? That's how hunters choose their game, based on their age and dignity. The elk with the largest rack is chosen to die so its head can hang in the den of some rich hunter. Half the time the hunters don't even take the meat from the game they shoot. They just leave it to rot.

31. This argument relies primarily on which of the following techniques to make its points?
   a. researched facts in support of an assertion
   b. emotional assertions
   c. fair and reasoned appeals to non-hunters
   d. fair and reasoned appeals to hunters

32. The author is most opposed to which of the following types of hunting?
   a. small game
   b. large game
   c. trophy
   d. elk

33. By choosing the term "shooting galleries," the author implies that
   a. the national forests have become dangerous for non-hunters
   b. hunters should satisfy themselves by taking pictures of animals
   c. hunters have an unfair advantage over prey in national forests
   d. hunting licenses cost little more than the pittance paid at carnival games

Improving Streamside Wildlife Habitats
(excerpt from Habitat Extension Bulletin put out by the Wyoming
Game and Fish Department)

Riparian vegetation [the green band of vegetation along a watercourse] can help stabilize stream banks; filter sediment from surface runoff; and provide wildlife habitat, livestock forage, and scenic value. Well-developed vegetation also allows bank soils to absorb extra water during spring runoff, releasing it later during drier months, thus improving late-summer stream flows.

In many parts of the arid West, trees and shrubs are found only in riparian areas. Woody plants are very important as winter cover for many wildlife species, including upland game birds such as pheasants and turkeys. Often this winter cover is the greatest single factor limiting game bird populations. Woody vegetation also provides hiding cover and browse for many other species of birds and mammals, both game and non-game.

Dead trees ("snags") are an integral part of streamside habitats and should be left standing whenever possible. Woodpeckers, nuthatches, brown creepers, and other birds eat the insects that decompose the wood. These insects usually pose no threat to nearby living trees. Occasionally a disease organism or misuse of pesticides will weaken or kill a stand of trees. If several trees in a small area begin to die, contact your local extension agent immediately.

34. What is the effect of the word choice "riparian"?
   a. It gives the article an authoritative, scientific tone.
   b. It causes confusion, since both streams and rivers could be viewed as riparian.
   c. It seems condescending, as if the author were stooping to teach readers.
   d. It misleads readers into thinking they are getting scientific information when they are not.

35. By listing the specific birds that live in riparian areas, the author conveys a sense of
   a. urgency on behalf of endangered species
   b. the rich and varied life in such areas
   c. his or her own importance as a scientific expert
   d. poetic wonder over the variety found in nature

36. Assume that the author has done some other writing on this topic for a different audience. The other piece begins: "Remember the last time you walked along a stream? No doubt thick vegetation prevented easy progress." What is the likely effect on the reader of this opening?
   a. an aroused interest, due to the reference to the reader's personal experience
   b. resentment, due to being addressed so personally
   c. loss of interest, because the opening line makes no attempt to draw the reader in
   d. confusion, because not every reader has walked along a stream

37. The main subject of the second paragraph of this passage is
   a. the types of birds that live in riparian areas
   b. the effect of winter cover on water purity
   c. the role of trees and shrubs in riparian areas
   d. how game bird populations are affected by winter cover

38. Overall, the assertions of this passage seem to be based on
   a. rash opinion with little observation behind it
   b. deeply held emotional convictions
   c. fact derived from scientific literature
   d. inconclusive evidence gathered in field studies

39. What does the word "arid" accomplish in the first sentence of the second paragraph?
   a. It provides a sense of the generally high altitude of the West.
   b. It signifies a change in subject from the Eastern U. S. to the West.
   c. It clarifies the author's purpose to discuss non-urban areas.
   d. It clarifies the reason that trees and shrubs are found only in riparian areas.

(excerpt from "First," a short story)

First, you ought to know that I'm "only" fourteen. My mother points this out frequently. I can make decisions for myself when I'm old enough to vote, she says. Second, I should tell you that she's right—I'm not always responsible. I sometimes take the prize for a grade-A dork. Last weekend, for instance, when I was staying at Dad's, I decided it was time I learned to drive. It was Sunday morning, 7 A. M. to be exact, and I hadn't slept well thinking about this argument I'll be telling you about in a minute. Nobody was up yet in the neighborhood, and I thought there would be no harm in backing the car out of the garage and cruising around the block. But Dad has a clutch car, and the "R" on the shift handle was up on the left side, awful close to first gear, and I guess you can guess the rest.

Dad's always been understanding. He didn't say, like Mom would, "Okay, little Miss Know-It-All, you can just spend the rest of the year paying this off." He worried about what might have happened to *me*—to *me*, you see, and that made me feel more guilty than anything. Overall, I just think he'd be a better number one caregiver, if you get my drift. Of course I can't say things like that to Mom.

To her, I have to say, "But Mom, Dad's place is closer to school. I could ride my bike."

She replies, "Jennifer Lynn, you don't own a bike, because you left it in the yard and it was stolen and you haven't got the perseverance it takes to do a little work and earn the money to replace it."

40. Which description best explains the structure of the story so far?
  a. chronological, according to what happens first, second, and so on
  b. reverse chronological order, with the most recent events recorded first
  c. intentionally confused order, incorporating flashbacks to previous events
  d. according to importance, with the most significant details related first

41. What device does the author use to illustrate the narrator's feelings about her mother and father?
  a. vivid and specific visual detail
  b. rhetorical questions, which make a point but don't invite a direct answer
  c. metaphors and other figurative language
  d. contrast between the parents' typical reactions

42. The narrator attributes her inability to sleep when staying at her father's house to
  a. thinking about a disagreement with someone
  b. the uncomfortable quiet of an early Sunday morning
  c. the sore throat she had from shouting so much
  d. her accident with the car

43. The first-person point of view in this story
  a. obscures how the narrator's mind works
  b. illustrates the thoughts and personality of the narrator
  c. makes the narrator seem distant and rigid
  d. gives us direct access to the minds of all the characters

44. When the narrator says she sometimes "take[s] the prize for a grade A dork," the word choice is intended to indicate
  a. that she doesn't know proper English
  b. her age and culture
  c. that she is unable to judge her own actions
  d. that she thinks she's better than most others who might be termed "dorks"

45. From the context in the last sentence of the passage, it can be determined that the word "perseverance" most nearly means
  a. attractiveness
  b. thinking ability
  c. ability to persist
  d. love of danger

46. Overall, this narrator's tone is best described as
  a. emotional and familiar
  b. stuck up and superior
  c. argumentative and tactless
  d. pleasant and reassuring

47. In choosing to use the bike argument with her mother, the narrator is trying to appeal to her mother's
  a. compassion over her lost bike
  b. disregard for material objects
  c. laziness
  d. reason

48. The main argument the narrator has been having with her mother is over whether she should
  a. be allowed to date
  b. live with her mother or father
  c. be allowed to drive a car
  d. pay for things she breaks

49. It appears that the mother has alienated her daughter by
   a. being too busy to give her the attention she needs
   b. having divorced her father
   c. insisting too much on reasonableness
   d. valuing things over people and feelings

50. What most likely happened with the car?
   a. The narrator mistook first gear for reverse and ran into the garage wall.
   b. The narrator stole it from her father and drove it over to her mother's.
   c. The father left it in gear, and when the narrator started it, it leapt forward into the wall.
   d. The narrator attempted suicide through carbon monoxide poisoning.

ANSWER KEY

If you miss any of the answers, you can find help for that kind of question in the lesson shown to the right of the answer.

1. c. Lesson 1
2. a. Lesson 1
3. d. Lesson 9
4. a. Lesson 16
5. b. Lesson 3
6. c. Lesson 12
7. c. Lesson 2
8. b. Lessons 6 and 7
9. a. Lesson 3
10. b. Lesson 8
11. d. Lesson 4
12. c. Lesson 17
13. d. Lesson 2
14. b. Lesson 8
15. c. Lesson 4
16. b. Lesson 13
17. a. Lesson 20
18. d. Lesson 3
19. c. Lesson 8
20. c. Lesson 20
21. b. Lesson 20
22. a. Lesson 16
23. c. Lesson 13
24. a. Lesson 14
25. b. Lesson 11

26. d. Lesson 9
27. c. Lesson 1
28. a. Lessons 6 and 10
29. d. Lesson 3
30. d. Lesson 6
31. b. Lesson 18
32. c. Lesson 2
33. c. Lesson 12
34. a. Lesson 12
35. b. Lesson 13
36. a. Lesson 11
37. c. Lesson 2
38. c. Lesson 4
39. d. Lesson 3
40. c. Lessons 6, 7, and 10
41. d. Lesson 8
42. a. Lesson 9
43. b. Lesson 11
44. b. Lesson 12
45. c. Lesson 3
46. a. Lesson 14
47. d. Lesson 18
48. b. Lesson 16
49. d. Lesson 17
50. a. Lesson 17

BUILDING A STRONG FOUNDATION

The truth is out there." If you're an "X-Files" fan, you've heard this eerie prophesy before. When agents Mulder and Scully arrive at the scene of a crime, they want to know the *truth* about what happened. They don't let the *opinions* of assuming police officers or disbelieving witnesses sway them; they want to know what people actually *saw* happen—to witness the tangible evidence themselves. With these collected *facts*, they retire to the lab or office to draw their own conclusions. Granted, these conclusions are sometimes a bit "out of this world," but the important thing is that the conclusions are based on facts, not the opinions of others.

You may never have thought of it this way before, but critical readers are a lot like special agents. When you read, you're looking for clues, not to solve a crime, but to understand the author's meaning. What is this passage about? What is the writer saying? What is his or her message? Sometimes you may feel that authors are trying to hide their meaning from you. But no matter how complex a piece of writing may be, the author always leaves plenty of clues for the careful reader to find. Your job as a reader is to find those clues. You can do this by being a good detective, opening your eyes and asking the right questions—in other words, by reading carefully and actively.

In these first five lessons, you'll cover the basics of reading comprehension. By the end of this section, you should be able to:

- Find the basic facts in a passage
- Determine the main idea of a passage
- Determine the meaning of unfamiliar words from context
- Distinguish between fact and opinion

GETTING THE ESSENTIAL INFORMATION

LESSON SUMMARY

The first step in increasing your reading comprehension is to learn how to get the basic information. Like a good detective, you start with the basic facts. To get the facts, you have to be an active reader, looking for clues in what you read.

magine, for a moment, that you are a detective. You have just been called to the scene of a crime; a house has been robbed. What's the first thing you should do when you arrive?

a. see what's on the TV
b. check what's in the fridge
c. get the basic facts of the case

The answer, of course, is **c**, get the basic facts of the case: the who, what, when, where, how, and why. What happened? To whom? When? Where? How did it happen? And why?

As a reader faced with a text, you go through a similar process. The first thing you should do is establish the facts. What does this piece of writing tell you? What happens? To whom? When, where, how, and why? If you can answer these basic questions, you're on your way to really comprehending what you read. (You'll work on answering the more difficult question—"*Why* did it happen?"—in Lesson 2.)

WHAT ARE THE FACTS?

Let's start with a definition. A **fact** is:

- Something that we know for certain to have happened
- Something that we know for certain to be true
- Something that we know for certain to exist

Much of what you read in college will be designed to provide you with facts. Whether it's a reading assignment in history, computer science, or criminal justice, you'll have to know how to pick out and make sense of important information. Sometimes this won't be so easy, especially when the reading is especially dense or complicated. To make it simpler, ask yourself these questions as you read: What facts am I expected to know? What am I to learn or be aware of? What happened? What is true? What exists?

PRACTICE PASSAGE 1

Jump right into the task of finding facts. The brief passage below is similar to something you might see in a newspaper. Read the passage carefully, and then answer the questions that follow. Remember, careful reading is active reading (see the Introduction), so mark up the text as you go. Underline key words and ideas; circle and define any unfamiliar words or phrases; record your reactions and questions in the margins.

On Tuesday, August 30, Mr. Blank, a prominent local citizen, arrived home from work to find that his apartment had been robbed. The thieves somehow managed to slip past building security at 131 West Elm Street with nearly all of Mr. Blank's belongings. In fact, the thieves left behind nothing but a stack of old *Home Decorator* magazines and a can of pork and beans. The robbery was reported by Mr. Blank's neighbor, who found Mr. Blank unconscious in his doorway. Apparently, Mr. Blank was so shocked by the robbery that he fainted. His neighbor immediately called an ambulance and then the police. Mr. Blank is now staying with relatives and is offering a reward of $25,000 for any information leading to the arrest of the thieves.

1. What happened to Mr. Blank?

2. When did it happen?

3. Where did it happen?

4. How did Mr. Blank react?

5. Who called the police?

6. What was left in the apartment?

Remember, good reading is active reading. Did you mark up the passage? If so, it may have looked something like this:

standing out; widely & popularly known

when | *who*

On Tuesday, August 30, Mr. Blank, a (prominent) local citizen, arrived home from work to find that his apartment had been robbed. The thieves somehow managed to slip past building security at 131 West Elm Street with nearly all of Mr. Blank's belongings. In fact, the thieves left behind nothing but a stack of old *Home Decorator* magazines and a can of pork and beans. The robbery was reported by Mr. Blank's neighbor, who found Mr. Blank unconscious in his doorway. Apparently, Mr. Blank was so shocked by the robbery that he fainted. His neighbor immediately called an ambulance and then the police. Mr. Blank is now staying with relatives and is offering a reward of $25,000 for any information leading to the arrest of the thieves.

} What happened – robbery

— where

how did they manage this?

interesting detail.

who else was involved

Wow!

lots of $!

You'll notice that the answers to the questions have all been underlined, because these are the key words and ideas in this passage. But here are the answers in a more conventional form:

1. What happened to Mr. Blank? *His apartment was robbed.*

2. When did it happen? *Sometime while Mr. Blank was at work on Tuesday, August 30.*

3. Where did it happen? *131 West Elm Street.*

4. How did Mr. Blank react? *He fainted.*

5. Who called the police? *Mr. Blank's neighbor.*

6. What was left in the apartment? *Some old* Home Decorator *magazines and a can of pork and beans.*

Notice that these questions went beyond the basic who, what, when, and where to include some of the details, like what was left in the apartment. This is because details in reading comprehension, as well as in detective work, can be very important clues that may help answer the remaining questions: who did it, how, and why.

PRACTICE PASSAGE 2

Here's another passage, this time something a little more like what someone might see at work. Read the passage carefully and answer the questions that follow:

To: All New Employees
From: Human Resources

In order for your first paycheck to be processed, we must have a number of documents completed and in our files. Once these documents are in our hands, you will be entered into our payroll system. These documents include: a completed company application; a W-4 form; an I-9 form; a Confidentiality Agreement, if applicable; an emergency contact sheet; and a copy of your resume. You should be sure all of these documents are filled out within your first week of work. In addition, we will need the following documents from you for your file to be complete: two letters of recommendation from previous employers, a high school and college transcript, and an insurance coverage application. We request that you complete your file within your first month of employment.

---

7. What papers must new employees have on file? List them below.

9. When should these circled items be completed?

10. When must the rest of the file be completed?

11. True or False: Everyone must sign a Confidentiality Agreement.

Before you look at the answers, look at the next page to see how you might have marked up the passage to highlight the important information.

8. In your list above, circle the items that employees must have on file in order to get paid.

To: All New Employees
From: Human Resources

In order for your first paycheck to be processed, we must have a number of documents completed and in our files. Once these documents are in our hands, you will be entered into our payroll system. These documents include: [a completed company application; a W-4 form; an I-9 form; a Confidentiality Agreement, if applicable; an emergency contact sheet; and a copy of your resume.] You should be sure all of these documents are filled out within your first week of work. In addition, we will need the following documents from you for your file to be complete: [two letters of recommendation from previous employers, a high school and college transcript, and an insurance coverage application.] We request that you complete your file within your first month of employment.

Important deadline!

Official copy of a student's educational record

Documents I need in order to get paid

Documents I need to complete file

Deadline for completing file

With a marked-up text like this, it's very easy to find the answers.

7. What papers must new employees have on file?

Company application

W-4 form

I-9 form

Confidentiality Agreement (if applicable)

Emergency contact sheet

Resume

Two letters of recommendation

High school and college transcripts

Insurance coverage application

8. In the list above, the items that employees must have on file in order to get paid are circled.

9. When should these circled items be completed? *Within the employee's first week of work.*

10. When must the rest of the file be completed? *Within the employee's first month of work.*

11. True or False: Everyone must sign a Confidentiality Agreement. *False; only those for whom it is "applicable."*

PRACTICE PASSAGE 3

Now look at one more short passage. Again, read carefully and then answer the questions that follow.

Today's postal service is more efficient and reliable than ever before. Mail that used to take months to move by horse and by foot now moves around the country in days or hours by truck, train, and plane. First class mail usually moves from New York City to Los Angeles in three days or less. If your letter or package is urgent, the U.S. Postal Service offers Priority Mail and Express Mail services. Priority Mail is guaranteed to go anywhere in the U.S. in two days or less. Express Mail will get your package there overnight.

12. Who or what is this passage about?

13. How was mail transported in the past?

14. How is mail transported now?

15. How long does first class mail take?

16. How long does Priority Mail take?

17. How long does Express Mail take?

Once again, here's how you might have marked up this passage:

---

then → Today's postal service is more efficient and reliable than ever before. Mail   *What a*
now →   that used to take <u>months</u> to move by <u>horse</u> and <u>by foot</u> now moves around the   *long time!*
            country in days or hours by <u>truck, train, and plane.</u> First class mail usually moves
            from New York City to Los Angeles in three days or less. If your letter or pack-   *3 services listed—*
Are there age is urgent, the U.S. Postal Service offers <u>Priority Mail</u> and <u>Express Mail</u> ser-   *First class—3 days*
other   vices. Priority Mail is guaranteed to go anywhere in the U.S. in two days or less.   *Priority—2 days*
services? Express Mail will get your package there overnight.   *Express—Overnight Fastest*

You can see how marking up a text helps make it easier to understand the information a passage conveys.

12. Who or what is this passage about? *The U.S. Postal Service.*

13. How was mail transported in the past? *By horse and foot.*

14. How is mail transported now? *By truck, train, and plane.*

15. How long does first class mail take? *Three days or less.*

16. How long does Priority Mail take? *Two days or less.*

17. How long does Express Mail take? *Overnight.*

SUMMARY

Active reading is the first essential step to comprehension. Why? Because active reading forces you to really *see* what you're reading, to look closely at what's there. Like a detective who arrives at the scene of a crime, if you look carefully and ask the right questions (who, what, when, where, how, and why), you're on your way to really comprehending what you read.

Skill Building Until Next Time

Below are some suggestions for practicing the skills covered in this chapter throughout the day and even the rest of the week. Try them!

- **Mark up** everything you read throughout the day—the newspaper, an assignment, a letter from a friend. Underline the key terms and ideas; circle and look up any unfamiliar words; write your reactions and questions in the margins. If possible, share these reactions with the writer and see if you can get answers to your questions.

- Develop a **"detective's eye."** Begin to notice things around you. Look at the details on people's faces; notice the architectural details of the buildings you enter. The more observant you are in daily life, the more enriched your life will be and the easier it will be to comprehend what you read.

L·E·S·S·O·N 2
FINDING THE MAIN IDEA

LESSON SUMMARY

A detective finds the facts to determine "whodunit" and what the motive was. A reader determines the facts not only for their own sake but also to find out why the author is writing: What's the main idea? This lesson shows you how to determine the main idea of what you read.

When Lesson 1 talked about establishing the facts—the who, what, when, where, and how—it omitted one very important question: Why? Now you're ready to tackle that all-important question. Just as there's a motive behind every crime, there's also a "motive" behind every piece of writing.

All writing is communication: A writer writes to convey his or her thoughts to an audience, the reader: you. Just as you have something to say (a motive) when you pick up the phone to call someone, writers have something to say (a motive) when they pick up a pen or pencil to write. Where a detective might ask, "Why did the butler do it?" the reader might ask, "Why did the author write this? What idea is he or she trying to convey?" What you're really asking is, "What is the writer's main idea?"

Finding the main idea is much like finding the motive of the crime. It's the motive of the crime (the *why*) that usually determines the other factors (the *who, what, when, where,* and *how*). Similarly, in writing, the main idea also determines the *who, what, when,* and *where* the writer will write about, as well as *how* he or she will write.

SUBJECT VS. MAIN IDEA

There's a difference between the *subject* of a piece of writing and its *main idea.* To see the difference, look again at the passage about the postal system. Don't skip over it! You read it in Lesson 1, but please read it again, and read it carefully.

> Today's postal service is more efficient and reliable than ever before. Mail that used to take months to move by horse and by foot now moves around the country in days or hours by truck, train, and plane. First class mail usually moves from New York City to Los Angeles in three days or less. If your letter or package is urgent, the U.S. Postal Service offers Priority Mail and Express Mail services. Priority Mail is guaranteed to go anywhere in the U.S. in two days or less. Express Mail will get your package there overnight.

You will often be asked in English class, "What is the main idea of this reading?"

For the passage above, you might be tempted to answer: "The post office."

But you'd be wrong.

This passage is *about* the post office, yes—but "the post office" is not the main idea of the passage. "The post office" is merely the *subject* of the passage (*who or what* the passage is about). The main idea must say something *about* this subject. The main idea of a text is usually an *assertion* about the subject. An assertion is a statement that requires evidence ("proof") to be accepted as true.

The main idea of a passage is an assertion about its subject, but it is something more: It is the idea that also holds together or controls the passage. The other sentences and ideas in the passage will all relate to that main idea and serve as "evidence" that the assertion is true. You might think of the main idea as a net that is cast over the other sentences. The main idea must be general enough to hold all of these ideas together.

Thus, the main idea of a passage is:

- An assertion about the subject
- The general idea that controls or holds together the paragraph or passage

Look at the postal service paragraph once more. You know what the subject is: "the post office." Now, see if you can determine the main idea. Read the passage again and look for the idea that makes an assertion about the postal service *and* holds together or controls the whole paragraph. Then answer the following question:

1. Which of the following sentences best summarizes the main idea of the passage?
   a. Express Mail is a good way to send urgent mail.
   b. Mail service today is more effective and dependable.
   c. First class mail usually takes three days or less.

Because a is specific—it tells us *only* about Express Mail—it cannot be the main idea. It does not encompass the rest of the sentences in the paragraph—it doesn't cover Priority Mail or first class mail. Answer c is also very specific. It tells us only about first class mail, so it, too, cannot be the main idea.

But b—"Mail service today is more effective and dependable"—*is* general enough to encompass the whole passage. And the rest of the sentences *support* the idea that this sentence asserts: Each sentence offers "proof" that the postal service today is indeed more efficient and reliable. Thus, the writer's motive is to tell us about the efficiency and reliability of today's postal service.

TOPIC SENTENCES

You'll notice that in the paragraph about the postal service, the main idea is expressed clearly in the first sentence: "Today's postal service is more efficient and reliable than ever before." A sentence, such as this one, that clearly expresses the main idea of a paragraph or passage is often called a *topic sentence*.

In many cases, as in the postal service paragraph, you will find the topic sentence at the beginning of the paragraph. You will also frequently find it at the end. Less often, but on occasion, the topic sentence may be found in the middle of the passage. Whatever the case may be, the topic sentence—like "Today's postal service is more efficient and reliable than ever before"—is an assertion, and it needs "proof." The proof is found in the facts and ideas that make up the rest of the passage. (Not all passages provide such a clear topic sentence that states the main idea. Less obvious passages will come up in later lessons.)

PRACTICE IN IDENTIFYING TOPIC SENTENCES

Remember that a topic sentence is a clear statement of the main idea of a passage; it must be general enough to encompass all of the ideas in that passage, and it usually makes an assertion about the subject of that passage. Knowing all that, you can answer the following question even without reading a passage.

Practice 1

2. Which of the following sentences is general enough to be a topic sentence?
   a. UNIX is one of the most common computer languages.
   b. There are many different computer languages.
   c. An old computer language is BASIC.
   d. Most IBM computers use OS/2.

The answer is **b**, "There are many different computer languages." Answers **a**, **c**, and **d** are all specific examples of what is said in **b**, so they are not general enough to be topic sentences.

Practice 2

Now look at the following paragraph. Underline the sentence that expresses the main idea, and notice how the other sentences work to support that main idea.

Erik always played cops and robbers when he was a boy; now, he's a police officer. Suzanne always played school as a little girl; today, she is a high school math teacher. Kara always played store; today, she owns a chain of retail clothing shops. Long before they are faced with the question, "What do you want to be when you grow up?" some lucky people know exactly what they want to do with their lives.

Which sentence did you underline? You should have underlined the *last* sentence: "Long before they are faced with that question 'What do you want to be when you grow up?' some lucky people know exactly what they want to do with their lives." This sentence is a good topic sentence; it expresses the idea that holds together the whole paragraph. The first three sentences—about Erik, Suzanne, and Kara—are *specific examples* of these lucky people. Notice that this time the topic sentence is found at the *end* of the paragraph.

Practice 3

Among the eight sentences below are *two* topic sentences. The other sentences are supporting sentences. Circle the two topic sentences. Then write the numbers of the supporting sentences that go with each topic sentence.

1. Furthermore, government employees receive terrific heath-care coverage.

2. Some police officer duties, like writing reports, have no risk at all.

3. For example, government employees have more paid holidays than employees of private companies.

4. Not all police duties are dangerous.

5. Others, like traffic duty, put police officers at very little risk.

6. Government employees enjoy numerous benefits.

7. Still other duties, like investigating accidents, leave officers free of danger.

8. In addition, government employees are well compensated for overtime hours.

Sentences 4 and 6 are the *two* topic sentences because both make an assertion about a general subject. The supporting sentences for topic sentence 4, "Not all police duties are dangerous," are sentences 2, 5, and 7. The supporting sentences for topic sentence 6, "Government employees enjoy numerous benefits," are the remaining sentences: 1, 3, and 8.

Here's how they look as paragraphs:

Not all police duties are dangerous. Some duties, like writing reports, have no risk at all. Others, like traffic duty, offer very little risk. Still other duties, like investigating accidents, leave officers free of danger.

Government employees enjoy numerous benefits. For example, they have more paid holidays than employees of private companies. In addition, they are well compensated for overtime hours. Furthermore, they receive terrific heath-care coverage.

You might have noticed the supporting sentences in the first paragraph about police duties begin with the following words: *some, others,* and *still other.* These words are often used to introduce examples. The second paragraph uses different words, but they have the same function: *for example, in addition,* and *furthermore.* If a sentence begins with such a word or phrase, that is a good indication it is *not* a topic sentence—because it is providing a specific example.

Here are some words and phrases often used to introduce specific examples:

for example	in particular
for instance	some
in addition	others
furthermore	

If you're having trouble finding the main idea of a paragraph, you might try eliminating the sentences that you know contain supporting evidence.

SUMMARY

Now you can answer the last of the questions—the *why*. What is the writer's motive? What's the main idea he or she wants to convey? By finding the sentence that makes an assertion about the subject of the paragraph and that encompasses the other sentences in the paragraph, you can uncover the author's motive.

Skill Building Until Next Time

- A paragraph, by definition, is a group of sentences about the same idea. As you read today and the rest of the week, notice how texts are divided into paragraphs. What idea holds each paragraph together? Can you identify any **topic sentences**?

- Formulate **topic sentences** about things that you come across in your day. Make assertions about these people, places, and things. For example, you may eat in the cafeteria every day. Make an *assertion* about it: "This cafeteria needs remodeling," for example. Or, make an assertion about a classmate: "June is a very hard worker," you might say. Then, support your assertions. What "evidence" could you supply for your paragraph? Why do you say the cafeteria needs remodeling? Is there paint peeling off the walls? Is it still decorated '60s style? Is it not wheelchair accessible? What evidence do you have that June is a hard worker? Is she always at the library? Does she ask informed questions in class? Does she look like she needs more sleep?

L·E·S·S·O·N 3

DEFINING VOCABULARY IN CONTEXT

LESSON SUMMARY

An active reader looks up unfamiliar words. But what if you don't have a dictionary? In a testing situation (or, for that matter, if you're reading on the bus) you almost certainly won't be able to look up words you don't know. Instead, you can use the context to help you determine the meaning.

S ometimes in your reading you come across words or phrases that are unfamiliar to you. You might be lucky enough to have a dictionary handy to look up that word or phrase, but what if you don't? How can you understand what you're reading if you don't know what all of the words mean? The answer is that you can use the rest of the passage, the *context*, to help you understand the new words.

FINDING MEANING FROM CONTEXT

Imagine you are a Hiring Supervisor at a large company. You have just received the following memorandum from the Human Resources Department. Read it carefully, marking it up as you go—but **don't** look up any unfamiliar words or phrases in a dictionary.

As you know, all new employees must have a Hiring Approval Form with salary specifications on file before they can be paid. In recent months several new employees have had their paychecks delayed because their Hiring Supervisors were remiss in filing the Hiring Approval Forms on time. Consequently, we are instituting a new policy. Beginning next week, if a Hiring Approval Form is not filed with Human Resources within one week of an employee's start date, that employee's first paycheck will be deducted from his or her Hiring Supervisor's paycheck. This amount will not be reimbursed unless the Hiring Supervisor submits the Hiring Approval Form within the following week. We're sorry if this seems like a draconian policy, but it is our only way to assure prompt payment of new employees.

As you read, you may have circled some words that are unfamiliar. Did you circle *remiss* and *draconian?* If so, don't look them up in a dictionary yet. If you do a little detective work, you can figure out what these words mean by looking carefully at how they are used in the paragraph.

WHAT DOES *REMISS* MEAN?

Start with *remiss.* How is this word used?

> In recent months several new employees have had their paychecks delayed because their Hiring Supervisors were *remiss* in filing the Hiring Approval Forms on time.

Even if you have no idea what *remiss* means, you can still tell something about the word by how it is used, by examining the words and ideas surrounding it. This is called determining word meaning through **context**.

Like detectives looking for clues at a crime scene, we must look at the passage for clues that will tell us what this word means.

So, given the sentence we have here, what can we tell about *remiss?* Well, because the Hiring Supervisors were *remiss,* several new employees didn't get their paychecks on time. That immediately tells us that *remiss* is *not* a good thing to be.

Furthermore, we know from this sentence that the Hiring Approval Forms must be filed by the Hiring Supervisors. That tells us that Hiring Supervisors were not doing something they were supposed to do, doesn't it? And as a result, the rest of the paragraph tells us, Hiring Supervisors will now be penalized for not filing the Hiring Approval Forms. Now you can take a pretty good guess at the meaning of *remiss.*

1. The Hiring Supervisors were *remiss* about the Hiring Approval Forms because they were

a. on time, prompt
b. negligent, irresponsible
c. incorrect, wrong

The correct answer, of course, is **b**. It certainly can't be **a**, because you know that the forms were late (the forms were not "on time"). Besides, you know *remiss* must mean something negative, since the Hiring Supervisors who continue to be remiss will be punished. Answer **c** is negative, but it doesn't make sense in the context of the sentence, which tells you the issue is time. Furthermore, you know **b** is the correct answer because you can substitute both *irresponsible* and *negligent* in the sentence instead of *remiss* and they both make sense.

Review: Finding Facts

Here's a quick review of what you learned in Lesson 1. If you're a Hiring Supervisor, you know that now you must be sure to get Hiring Approval Forms in on *time*. But when is *on time*?

2. When must the Hiring Approval Form be in for the new employee to be paid on time?
a. within one week of the employee's start date
b. by next week
c. within one month of the hiring approval

A quick check of the facts in the paragraph will tell you the answer: **a**, within one week of the employee's start date.

WHAT DOES *DRACONIAN* MEAN?

Look again at the sentence in which *draconian* is used:

We're sorry if this seems like a *draconian* policy, but it is our only way to assure prompt payment of new employees.

Again, even if you have no idea what *draconian* means (and no, it has nothing to do with Dracula!), you can still tell what kind of word it is by the way it is used. You can, for example, answer this question:

3. *Draconian* is a
a. positive word
b. negative word

The answer, of course, is that it is a negative word. How can you tell? Well, there's one very obvious clue in the sentence: "We're sorry." Why would the memo writers be sorry if *draconian* was something to be happy about?

Okay, now that you've established that *draconian* is not something good, figure out *why* by determining exactly what it means. Your first clue to the meaning of *draconian* was "We're sorry." What other clues can you find? Look at how *draconian* is being used in this sentence: It is used to describe the new policy explained in the memo. And what is this new policy? The Hiring Supervisor's pay will be deducted if he or she doesn't make sure the Hiring Approval Form is completed within one week of a new employee's start date. And if the Hiring Approval Form still isn't filed by the end of the next week, the Hiring Supervisor will *not* be reimbursed. That should give you a pretty good idea of what *draconian* means.

4. A *draconian* policy is one that is
a. mismanaged, unorganized
b. lenient, light
c. drastic, severe
d. smart, wise

The correct answer, of course, is **c**, "drastic, severe." It can't be **b** or **d**, because these are positive things that the writers of the memo wouldn't be sorry for. And **a** is not an appropriate answer because, as you can see, the policy is quite clear; you know exactly what form needs to be on file, who's responsible for it, and what happens if the form is not filed. In addition, you can tell that **c** is the right answer because docking someone's pay without reimbursement because of missing paperwork certainly is a harsh measure.

By the way, the word *draconian* comes from the ancient Greek lawmaker, Draco, who wrote particularly harsh laws with severe penalties.

HOW MUCH CONTEXT DO YOU NEED?

In the previous example, you would still be able to understand the main message of the memorandum even if you didn't know—or couldn't figure out—the meaning of *remiss* and *draconian*. In some cases, however, your understanding of a passage depends on your understanding of a particular word or phrase. Can you understand the following sentence, for example, without knowing what *adversely* means?

The new policy will *adversely* affect all employees.

If you're an employee, you certainly want to know how you're going to be affected. What does *adversely* mean? Is it something good or bad? As good a detective as you may be, there simply aren't enough clues in this sentence to tell you what this word means. But a passage with more information will give you what you need to determine meaning from context.

The new policy will *adversely* affect all employees. It will freeze their pay, limit their vacation time, and reduce their health benefits.

5. In the passage, *adversely* most nearly means
   a. mildly, slightly
   b. regularly, steadily
   c. negatively, unfavorably
   d. immediately, swiftly

The correct answer is **c**, "negatively, unfavorably." The brief passage now tells you exactly what the policy will do to the employees: It will freeze their pay, limit their vacations, and reduce their benefits. It certainly is not **a**, a slight or mild change, nor is it **b**, a regular or steady change. And you don't know if it is an immediate or swift change (**d**), because the sentence says nothing about the time frame in which this change will take place. Remember, good detectives don't make assumptions they can't support with facts; and there are no facts in this sentence to support the assumption that the changes will take place immediately. Thus, **c** is the best answer.

You may also have noticed that *adversely* is very similar to the word *adversary*. And if you know that an *adversary* is a hostile opponent or enemy, then you know that *adversely* cannot be something positive. Or, if you know the word *adversity*—hardship or misfortune—then you know that *adversely* must mean something negative or difficult. All of these words share the same root—*advers*. Only the endings change.

PRACTICE

Read the following passages and determine the meaning of the words from their context. The answers appear immediately after the questions.

Although social work is not a particularly *lucrative* career, I wouldn't do anything else. Knowing I'm helping others is far more important to me than money.

6. *Lucrative* means
   a. highly profitable
   b. highly rewarding
   c. highly exciting

When you are in an interview, try not to show any *overt* signs that you are nervous. Don't shift in your chair, shake, or stutter.

7. *Overt* means
   a. embarrassing, awkward
   b. subtle, suggestive
   c. obvious, not hidden

By the time our staff meeting ended at 8:00, I was *ravenous*. I had skipped lunch and hadn't eaten since breakfast.

8. *Ravenous* means
   a. like a raven, bird-like
   b. extremely hungry, greedy for food
   c. exhausted, ready for bed

Answers

6. a. The writer says money is not important to him. If money is not an issue, it is okay that social work is not *highly profitable*, that it doesn't earn a lot of money.

7. c. Shifting, shaking, and stuttering are all *obvious, not hidden* signs of nervousness. They are not **b**, subtle or suggestive; and though they may make the interviewee feel **a**, embarrassed or awkward, the signs themselves are not embarrassing or awkward.

8. b. Because the writer hadn't eaten since breakfast, she is *extremely hungry, greedy for food*. She may also be **c**, exhausted, but the context tells us that this word has something to do with eating.

SUMMARY

Being able to determine the meaning of unfamiliar words from their context is an essential skill for reading comprehension. Sometimes there will be unfamiliar words whose meaning you can't figure out without a dictionary. But more often than not, a careful look at the context will give you enough clues to meaning.

Skill Building Until Next Time

■ Circle any unfamiliar words you come across today and the rest of the week. Instead of looking them up in a dictionary, try to figure out the meanings of these words from their context. Then look them up in a dictionary to make sure you are correct.

■ Begin a vocabulary list of the words you look up as you work your way through this book. Many people feel insecure about their reading and writing skills because they have a limited vocabulary. The more words you know, the easier it will be to understand what others are saying and to express what you have to say. By writing these new words down, you'll help seal them in your memory.

L·E·S·S·O·N 4

THE DIFFERENCE BETWEEN FACT AND OPINION

LESSON SUMMARY

In order to make sense of what you read, you have to be able to tell whether you're reading fact or opinion. This lesson tells you how to distinguish what someone knows for certain from what someone believes.

What's the difference between fact and opinion, and what does it matter, anyway? It matters a great deal, especially when it comes to reading comprehension.

During your college career, you'll be exposed to a wide variety of literature, ranging from analytical articles based on cold hard facts to fictional novels that arise wholly from the author's imagination. However, much of what you read will be a mixture of facts and the author's opinions. Part of becoming a critical reader means realizing that opinions are not evidence; for opinions to be valid, they must be supported by cold, hard **facts**:

- Things *known* for certain to have happened
- Things *known* for certain to be true
- Things *known* for certain to exist

　　Opinions, on the other hand, are:

- Things *believed* to have happened
- Things *believed* to be true
- Things *believed* to exist

As you can see, the key difference between fact and opinion lies in the difference between *believing* and *knowing*. Opinions may be based on facts, but they are still what we *think*, not what we *know*. Opinions are debatable; facts are not.

USING FACTS TO SUPPORT OPINIONS

Reasonable opinions are those that are *based on fact*; and indeed, that is what much of writing is: the writer's opinion (an assertion about his or her subject) supported by facts or other evidence.

Think about the topic sentences you formed after you finished Lesson 2. Did you form a topic sentence about a classmate, for example? Perhaps you made an assertion like this:

James is a great student.

This sentence is a good topic sentence; it's an assertion about the subject, James. And it is also an opinion. It is, after all, debatable; someone could just as easily take the opposite position and say:

James is a terrible student.

This is another good topic sentence, and it's another opinion. Now, a good writer will show his or her readers that this opinion is *valid* by supporting it with facts. For example:

James is a great student. He always asks well-informed questions in class. His books are marked up with highlighter and comments in the margins, so I know he does his reading. He hands his papers in on time, every time. And he even meets with the professor after class to discuss the material further.

Notice how the topic sentence states an opinion, whereas the rest of the sentences support that opinion

with facts about how James acts as a student. Now, that is a much more effective paragraph than something like this:

James is a terrible student. I don't think he's very smart. He's so lazy and never sits up straight. Everything he says is a bunch of baloney anyway.

Why is the first paragraph so much better? Because it's not just opinion. It's opinion supported by fact, evidence. The second paragraph is all opinion. Every sentence is debatable; every sentences tells us what the author *thinks* is true, but not what is *known* to be true. The author of the second paragraph doesn't provide any evidence to support why he thinks that James is such a lousy student. As a result, we're not likely to take his opinion very seriously.

In the first paragraph, on the other hand, the writer offers concrete evidence for why she thinks James is a great student. After the initial opinion, she provides facts—specific things James does (which can be verified by other observers) that make him a good student. You may still not agree that James is a great student, but at least you can see exactly why this writer thinks so.

DISTINGUISHING FACT FROM OPINION

When you read academic materials very often you will have to distinguish between fact and opinion—between what the writer thinks and how the writer supports what he or she thinks, between what is proven to be true and what needs to be proved.

A good test for whether something is a fact or opinion might be to ask yourself, "Can this statement be debated? Is this known for certain to be true?" If you answer *yes* to the first question, you have an opinion; if you answer *yes* to the second, you have a fact.

PRACTICE 1

Try these questions on the following statements. Read them carefully, and then write F in the blank if the statement is a fact and O if it is an opinion. The answers appear right after the questions.

_____ **1.** The Olympics are held every two years.

_____ **2.** The Olympics are really fun to watch.

_____ **3.** The Olympics should be held every year.

_____ **4.** The 1996 Summer Olympics were held in Atlanta, Georgia.

_____ **5.** The long jump is the most exciting Olympic event.

Answers

1. Fact

2. Opinion

3. Opinion

4. Fact

5. Opinion

PRACTICE 2

Now try the same exercise but with a complete paragraph. <u>Underline</u> the facts and use a highlighter or colored pen to highlight the opinions. Be careful—you may find fact and opinion together in the same sentence. When you've finished, you can check your answers against the marked passage that follows.

There are many different ways to invest your money to provide for a financially secure future. Many people invest in stocks and bonds, but I think good old-fashioned savings accounts and CDs (certificates of deposit) are the best way to invest your hard-earned money. Stocks and bonds are often risky, and it doesn't make sense to risk losing the money you've worked so hard for. True, regular savings accounts and CDs can't make you a millionaire overnight or provide the high returns some stock investments do. But by the same token, savings accounts and CDs are fully insured and provide steady, secure interest on your money. That makes a whole lot of cents.

Answers

How did you do? Was it easy to distinguish between the facts and the opinions? Here's what your marked-up passage should look like. The facts are underlined and the opinions are in boldface type.

> There are many different ways to invest your money to provide for a financially secure future. Many people invest in stocks and bonds, **but I think good old-fashioned savings accounts and CDs (certificates of deposit) are the best way to invest your hard-earned money.** Stocks and bonds are often risky, **and it doesn't make sense to risk losing the money you've worked so hard for.** True, regular savings accounts and CDs can't make you a millionaire overnight or provide the high returns some stock investments do. But by the same token, savings accounts and CDs are fully insured and provide steady, secure interest on your money. **That makes a whole lot of cents.**

PRACTICE 3

To strengthen your ability to distinguish between fact and opinion, try this. Take a fact, such as:

FACT: *Wednesday is the fourth day of the week.*

Now, turn it into an opinion. Make it something debatable, like this:

OPINION: *Wednesday is the longest day of the week.*

Here's another example:

FACT: *People insured by an HMO can only choose from doctors on that HMO plan.*

OPINION: *People insured by HMOs should be able to choose any doctor they wish.*

Now you try. Some suggested answers come after the questions.

6. **FACT:** *In the United States, you must be at least 21 years of age to drink alcohol.*

OPINION:

7. **FACT:** *There have been many proposals recently for a flat income tax.*

OPINION:

8. **FACT:** *Affirmative action programs have recently been eliminated.*

OPINION:

9. FACT: *Many companies have dress-down days on Fridays.*

OPINION:

10. FACT: *Several states have recently raised their highway speed limits from 55 miles per hour to 65 miles per hour or more.*

OPINION:

Answers

There are, of course, many opinions you could form from these subjects. Here are some possible answers:

6. The legal drinking age should be 18.
There should be no age requirement for drinking alcohol.
You should not be able to drink alcohol until you're 25.

7. There should be a flat income tax of 20 percent.
A flat income tax rate would be disastrous.

All people who earn more than $100,000 a year should have a flat tax of 25 percent; people who earn less should not be taxed at all.

8. Affirmative action was a terrific program that should not have been eliminated.
It's about time we got rid of affirmative action.

9. Dress-down days improve employee morale.
Dress-down days make workers less productive.
Companies should allow their employees to dress however they wish.

10. Speed limits should remain 55 miles per hour.
There should be no speed limit at all.

SUMMARY

Being able to differentiate between fact and opinion is a very important skill. Like a detective, you need to know the difference between what people *think* and what people *know*, between what people *believe* to be true and what has been *proven* to be true. Then you will be able to see whether writers support their opinions, and, if they do, how they do it. Then you will be able to judge for yourself the validity of those opinions.

Skill Building Until Next Time

- Listen carefully to what people say today and try to determine whether they are stating a fact or expressing an opinion. When they offer opinions, do they support them?
- As you come across facts and opinions today, practice turning them into their opposites; make facts out of opinions and opinions out of facts.

L·E·S·S·O·N 5

PUTTING IT ALL TOGETHER

LESSON SUMMARY

This lesson reviews what you learned in Lessons 1–4: getting the facts, finding the main idea, determining what words mean in context, and distinguishing between fact and opinion. In this lesson, you'll get vital practice in using all four skills at once.

In order to solve a crime, a detective cannot *just* get the facts of the case, *just* discover the motive, *just* decipher difficult clues, or *just* distinguish between fact and opinion. To be successful, a detective must do all of these things at once. Similarly, reading really can't be broken down into these separate tasks. Reading comprehension comes from employing all of these strategies at once. So this lesson gives you the opportunity to put all these strategies together and take your reading comprehension skills to the next level.

REVIEW: WHAT YOU'VE LEARNED SO FAR

These are the strategies you studied in the past four lessons:

- **Lesson 1: Finding the facts in what you read.** You practiced looking for the basic information that was being conveyed in the paragraphs: the who, what, when, where, and how.

- **Lesson 2: Finding the main idea.** You learned about topic sentences and how they express an assertion about the subject of the paragraph. You saw how the main idea must be general enough to encompass all of the other sentences in the paragraph; it is the thought that controls the paragraph, and the other sentences work to support that main idea.

- **Lesson 3: Determining the meaning of words from context.** You practiced looking for clues to meaning in the words and sentences surrounding the unfamiliar word or phrase.

- **Lesson 4: Distinguishing between fact and opinion.** You learned that a fact is something *known* to be true, whereas an opinion is something *believed* to be true. You practiced distinguishing between the two and saw how good paragraphs use facts to support opinions.

If any of these terms or strategies sound unfamiliar to you, STOP. Take a few minutes to review whatever lesson is unclear.

PRACTICE

In this lesson, you will sharpen your reading comprehension skills by using all of the above strategies at once. This will become more natural to you as your reading skills develop.

PRACTICE PASSAGE 1

Begin by looking at the following paragraph. Remember to read actively; mark up the text as you go. Then answer the questions. An example of how to mark up the passage, as well as the answers to the questions, follow the questions.

Following proper procedure is important in any job. But in no job is following proper procedure more important than in police work. In police work, not following proper procedure—like not handling evidence properly—can cause an officer to ruin a case by destroying an important clue. Later, the officer may be unable to convict the perpetrator in court because of mishandled evidence. Furthermore, not following proper procedure at the scene of an accident or hold-up, for example, could cause innocent people to get hurt. Most importantly, not following proper procedure in dangerous situations like robberies in progress and high-speed chases can cost an officer his or her life.

1. What is the subject of this passage?

2. According to the passage, which of the following consequences can happen to a police officer who doesn't follow proper procedure? (Circle all correct answers.)
   a. lose his or her job
   b. ruin the court case
   c. be unable to solve the case
   d. get a reduction in pay
   e. lose his or her life
   f. cause others to get hurt
   g. get transferred

3. A *perpetrator* is
   a. a victim of a crime
   b. a committer of a crime
   c. an investigator of a crime
   d. the object stolen

4. Which of the following best summarizes the main idea of the passage?
   a. You will get fired if you don't follow proper procedure.
   b. A police officer's life depends upon proper procedure.
   c. Police officers more than anyone else must follow proper procedure.

5. True or False: "But in no job is following proper procedure more important than in police work" is a topic sentence.

6. True or False: "But in no job is following proper procedure more important than in police work" is an opinion.

Marking Practice Passage 1

Before you check the answers, look again at the paragraph. Did you mark it up? If so, it may look something like this:

What can happen–
–ruin a case (destroy clue)
–mishandle evidence (unable to convict)
–hurt innocent people
–get killed

Following proper procedure is important in any job. But in no job is following proper procedure more important than in police work. In police work, not following proper procedure—like not handling evidence properly—can cause an officer to ruin a case by destroying an important clue. Later, the officer may be unable to convict the (perpetrator) in court because of mishandled evidence. Furthermore, not following proper procedure at the scene of an accident or hold up, for example, could cause innocent people to get hurt. Most importantly, not following proper procedure in dangerous situations like robberies in progress and high-speed chases can cost an officer his or her life.

main idea

perpetrator: person who carried out or commits a crime

Answers

1. The subject of the paragraph is *following proper police procedure.* Remember, the subject of a passage is who or what the passage is about.

2. b, c, e, f. These results are all mentioned in the passage. A police officer who doesn't follow proper procedure may lose his or her job (a), get a reduc-

tion in pay (d), or get transferred (g), but none of these consequences are mentioned *in the paragraph itself.*

Remember, you're looking for the facts that the *author* has provided. It is extremely important, especially in test situations, not to put in an answer that isn't there in the text. *Logic* may tell you that an officer who doesn't follow proper procedure may lose his or her job, but the paragraph doesn't tell you this. Like a good detective, you need to stick to the facts of the case: what's in the passage before you. Any assumption that you make about a passage must be grounded in evidence found *in that passage itself.*

3. **b.** A *perpetrator* is a person who commits a crime. The most obvious clue is the way the word is used in the sentence: "the officer may be unable to convict the perpetrator in court." The officer wouldn't want to convict anyone but the person who committed the crime.

4. **c.** Answer **a** is an assumption that is not based on anything written in the passage. Answer **b** is too specific—it is only one example of what happens to an officer who doesn't follow proper procedure. Not all cases of not following proper procedure could cost an officer his or her life. Only **c** is general enough to encompass the whole paragraph.

5. **True.** This sentence expresses the main idea.

6. **True.** This sentence is an opinion; it is debatable. Someone else might think that it is more important for a firefighter to follow proper procedure;

someone else might say it's more important for a construction worker to follow proper procedure. This is clearly what the writer thinks, not an established fact.

How did you do? If you got all six answers correct, congratulations! If you missed one or more questions, check the table below to see which lessons to review.

If you missed:	Then study:
Question 1	Lesson 2
Question 2	Lesson 1
Question 3	Lesson 3
Question 4	Lesson 2
Question 5	Lesson 2
Question 6	Lesson 4

PRACTICE PASSAGE 2

Try one more paragraph to conclude this first section. Once again, mark up the paragraph carefully and then answer the questions that follow.

Almost half of all Americans do not have health-care coverage. Those who do have coverage often pay exorbitant rates for their insurance. A young, healthy married couple in New York City, for example, must pay $359 per month to have only basic coverage from U.S. Healthcare; that coverage does not include eye care or dental care. Furthermore, this couple can only use U.S. Healthcare doctors. Most other HMOs (Health Maintenance Organizations) have similar programs that charge hard-working citizens outrageous fees for limited services. Even the most basic Medicare coverage through Blue Cross/Blue Shield costs a single adult over $600 a year—and this plan includes hundreds of dollars in deductibles. Americans need more adequate and affordable health-care coverage.

7. According to the passage, how many Americans have heath-care coverage?

    a. all

    b. about one-third

    c. about one-half

8. A married couple in New York City must pay $359 to U.S. Healthcare

    a. each week

    b. each month

    c. each year

9. True or False: The U.S. Healthcare plan described does not include dental care.

10. U.S. Healthcare's plan allows patients to choose

    a. any doctor they wish

    b. any HMO doctor they wish

    c. among U.S. Healthcare doctors only

11. *Exorbitant* means

    a. extremely small

    b. excessive, unreasonable

    c. reasonable, appropriate

12. The main idea of this paragraph is best expressed in which sentence in the paragraph?

13. Indicate whether the following sentences are *fact* or *opinion*:

    a. "Those who do have coverage often pay exorbitant rates for their insurance."

    b. "Furthermore, this couple can only use U.S. Healthcare doctors."

    c. "Americans need more adequate and affordable heath-care coverage."

Answers

7. c. See the first sentence.

8. b. See the third sentence.

9. True. See the third sentence.

10. c. See the fourth sentence.

11. b. There are several context clues. One is the use of the term *outrageous* in the fifth sentence to describe the heath-care fees. Also, the last sentence complains that heath care is not "affordable." Furthermore, the example the writer gives immediately after using the term *exorbitant*—$359 a month—shows that this word cannot mean **a**, *small*, and the use of the word *outrageous* shows that **c**, *reasonable*, cannot be the correct answer.

12. The last sentence. The point of the whole passage is that "Americans need more adequate and affordable heath-care coverage."

13. Choice **a** is **opinion.** It is debatable whether the fees are exorbitant.

    Choice **b** is **fact.** This is verifiable information.

    Choice **c** is **opinion.** This is a debatable proposition.

    How did you do this time? Better? If you missed any questions, this time *you* figure out which questions correspond with which lessons. This will help you see what categories you most need help with.

Skill Building Until Next Time

- Review the Skill Building sections from each lesson this week. Try any Skill Builders you didn't already do.
- Write a paragraph about what you've learned in this section. Begin your paragraph with a clear topic sentence, like: "I've learned several reading strategies since Lesson 1" or "I've learned that reading comprehension isn't as difficult as I thought." Then, write several sentences that support or explain your assertion. Try to use at least one vocabulary word that you've learned in this section.

STRUCTURE

Now that you've covered the basics, you can begin to focus on one specific reading comprehension strategy: structure. How do writers organize their ideas?

You might want to think of a writer as an architect. Every building has a number of rooms. But how these rooms are arranged is up to the architect. The same goes for a piece of writing—how the sentences and ideas are arranged is entirely up to the writer. However, most architects—and most writers—generally follow certain patterns, not because they can't think on their own, but because these patterns work. In this section, you'll study four organizational patterns that work for writers:

- Chronological order
- Order of importance
- Compare and contrast
- Cause and effect

You'll learn to recognize these patterns and some of the reasons why writers use them.

START FROM THE BEGINNING: CHRONOLOGICAL ORDER

6

LESSON SUMMARY

This lesson focuses on one of the simplest structures writers use: chronological order, or arrangement of events by the order in which they occured.

There are many ways to tell a story. Some stories start in the middle and flash backward to the beginning; a few start at the end and tell the story in reverse. But most of the time, stories start at the beginning. Writers often begin with what happened first and then tell what happened next, and next, and so on until the end. When writers tell a story in this order, from beginning to end in the order in which things happened, they are telling it in *chronological* order. *Chronology* is the arrangement of events in the order in which they occurred.

CHRONOLOGY AND TRANSITIONS

Much of what you read is arranged in chronological order. Newspaper and magazine articles, minutes of meetings, explanations of procedures, and so on are usually arranged this way. For example, look at the following paragraph that might be found in a company newsletter:

> This year's employee award ceremony was a tremendous success. The first award was given to Carlos Fe for Perfect Attendance. The second award, for Most Dedicated Employee, went to Jennifer Steele. Then our president, Martin Lucas, interrupted the awards ceremony to announce that he and his wife were having a baby. When he finished, everyone stood up for a congratulatory toast. Afterward, the third award was given to Karen Hunt for Most Inspiring Employee. Finally, President Lucas ended the ceremony by giving everyone a bonus check for $100.

You'll notice that this paragraph tells what happened at the ceremony from start to finish. You'll also notice that you can tell the order in which things happened in two ways. First, you can tell by the order of the sentences themselves—first things first, last things last. Second, you can tell by the use of *transitional words and phrases*, which signal a shift from one idea to the next. Here is the same paragraph with the transitional words underlined:

> This year's employee award ceremony was a tremendous success. The <u>first</u> award was given to Carlos Fe for Perfect Attendance. The <u>second</u> award, for Most Dedicated Employee, went to Jennifer Steele. <u>Then</u> the president, Martin Lucas, interrupted the awards ceremony to announce that he and his wife were having a baby. <u>When</u> he finished, everyone stood up for a congratulatory toast. <u>Afterward</u>, the <u>third</u> award was given to Karen Hunt for Most Inspiring

Employee. <u>Finally</u>, President Lucas ended the ceremony by giving everyone a bonus check for $100.

The underlined words—*first, second, then, when, afterward, third*, and *finally*—are transitional words that keep these events linked together in chronological order. Look at how the paragraph sounds without these words:

> This year's employee award ceremony was a tremendous success. The award was given to Carlos Fe for Perfect Attendance. The award for Most Dedicated Employee went to Jennifer Steele. The president, Martin Lucas, interrupted the awards ceremony to announce that he and his wife were having a baby. He finished; everyone stood up for a congratulatory toast. The award was given to Karen Hunt for Most Inspiring Employee. President Lucas ended the ceremony by giving everyone a bonus check for $100.

It doesn't sound quite as good, does it?

PRACTICE WITH TRANSITIONAL WORDS AND PHRASES

PRACTICE PASSAGE 1

Here's a more extreme example of a paragraph with the transitional words and phrases omitted:

> I went to work early to get some extra filing done. I got there; the phone started ringing. My boss walked in. He asked me to type up a letter for him. He asked me to make arrangements for a client to stay in town overnight. I looked at my watch; it was already 11 o'clock.

Now, take the paragraph and add the following transitional words and phrases:

immediately	yesterday
as soon as	a moment later
when	then

_____ I went to work early to get some extra filing done. _____ I got there, the phone started ringing. _____ my boss walked in. _____ he asked me to type up a letter for him. _____ he asked me to make arrangements for a client to stay in town overnight. _____ I looked at my watch, it was already 11 o'clock.

See how much better the paragraph sounds with transitional words and phrases to guide you?

Answers

You might have come up with a slightly different version, but here's one good way to fill in the blanks:

Yesterday I went to work early to get some extra filing done. As soon as I got there, the phone started ringing. A moment later my boss walked in. Immediately he asked me to type up a letter for him. Then he asked me to make arrangements for a client to stay in town overnight. When I looked at my watch, it was already 11 o'clock.

PRACTICE PASSAGE 2

Here is a series of events listed in random order. Use the transitional words and phrases in each sentence to help you put them in proper chronological order. Number the sentences from 1–6 in the blank provided.

_____ *Once* the investigation is complete, you will be ranked.

_____ If you pass the exam, you must *then* have an oral interview.

_____ In order to become a corrections officer in Texas, you must complete several steps.

_____ *After* your interview has been scored, your background will be investigated.

_____ *Finally*, after you are accepted, you must take 120 hours of classroom instruction.

_____ *First*, you must take a written examination.

Answers

You should have numbered the blanks in this order: 5, 3, 1, 4, 6, 2. Here's how the sentences look together in a paragraph:

In order to become a corrections officer in Texas, you must complete several steps. First, you must take a written examination. If you pass the exam, you must then have an oral interview. After your interview has been scored, your background will be investigated. Once the investigation is complete, you will be ranked. Finally, after you are accepted, you must take 120 hours of classroom instruction.

PRACTICE PASSAGE 3

Remember the story of Mr. Blank, who came home to find that his apartment had been robbed? On the next page is the way his story was presented in Lesson 1.

On Tuesday, August 30, Mr. Blank, a prominent local citizen, arrived home from work to find his apartment had been robbed. The thieves somehow managed to slip past building security at 131 West Elm Street with nearly all of Mr. Blank's belongings. In fact, the thieves left behind nothing but a stack of old *Home Decorator* magazines and a can of pork and beans. The robbery was reported by Mr. Blank's neighbor, who found Mr. Blank unconscious in his doorway. Apparently Mr. Blank was so shocked by the robbery that he fainted. His neighbor immediately called an ambulance and then the police. Mr. Blank is now staying with relatives and is offering a reward of $25,000 for any information leading to the arrest of the thieves.

Notice that this paragraph is *not* arranged in chronological order. Take the ten different events that make up the story and rearrange them so that they are in chronological order.

Here's the order of events as they are presented in the story:

- Mr. Blank came home.
- His apartment was robbed.
- Thieves slipped by building security with his things.
- Thieves left only magazines and a can of pork and beans behind.
- Mr. Blank's neighbor reported the robbery.
- Mr. Blank was found by his neighbor.
- Mr. Blank fainted.
- Mr. Blank's neighbor called an ambulance.
- Mr. Blank's neighbor called the police.
- Mr. Blank offered a reward.

Now put the events in chronological order.

1.

2.

3.

4.

5.

6.

7.

8.

9.

10.

Now, take these chronologically ordered events and make them into a cohesive paragraph. To do this, you need to add transitional words and phrases. Here is a list of transitional words and phrases often used in chronologically organized passages:

first	soon
second	after
third	before
next	during
now	while
then	meanwhile
when	in the meantime
as soon as	at last
immediately	eventually
suddenly	finally

Write your paragraph, putting the events in chronological order with transitional phrases, below or on a separate piece of paper.

Answers

There are, of course, many possible ways of using transitional words and phrases to put Mr. Blank's story in chronological order. One paragraph might look like this:

> On Tuesday, Mr. Blank's apartment was robbed by thieves who slipped past building security with almost all Mr. Blank's things <u>while</u> Mr. Blank was at work. The thieves left only some magazines and a can of pork and beans behind. <u>When</u> Mr. Blank came home, he was so upset that he fainted. <u>Soon</u> Mr. Blank was found by his neighbor. His neighbor <u>immediately</u> called an ambulance and <u>then</u> called the police to report the robbery. Mr. Blank is <u>now</u> offering a $25,000 reward.

PRACTICE PASSAGE 4

Chronological order is very important, especially when it comes to procedures. If you perform the steps out of chronological order, you won't get the results you desire. Just imagine, for example, that you are trying to bake a cake. What happens when you do things out of order? You go without dessert.

Of course, the consequences of not following proper chronological order at work and school can be much more serious, so it's important that you strengthen this skill. Read the following paragraph, marking it up to help you keep track of the steps that an employee must follow in order to get tuition reimbursement.

> Our company will be happy to reimburse you for college courses that enhance your job performance. Before you register for the course, you must get approval first from your immediate supervisor and then from Human Resources. If you are taking the course for credit, you must receive a C+ or better in the course. If you are not taking it for credit, you must pass the course. After you have completed the course, you must write a report explaining the content of the course and its relevance to your position. Then, you must fill out a reimbursement request. Attach a tuition payment receipt, your report, and a copy of your grades to this request and promptly submit this request to your supervisor. Once your supervisor has approved the request, you can then submit all of these forms to Human Resources, and you should receive your check within two weeks.

There are eight separate steps an employee must take in order to be reimbursed for college course work. What are they? List them below in the order in which the employee must do them.

1.

2.

3.

4.

5.

6.

7.

8.

If you marked up your paragraph, you should easily see the different steps. Here's how you might have marked it up. The transitional words and phrases are highlighted in bold.

Our company will be happy to reimburse you for college courses that ~~need approval before registering!~~

enhance your job performance. **Before** you register for the course, you must get

1 + 2 approval **first** from your immediate supervisor and **then** from Human Resources.

1st –get supervisor approval

3 If you are taking the course for credit, you must receive a C+ or better in the

2nd –get HR approved

course. If you are not taking it for credit, you must pass the course. **After** you

3rd –take course– get C+ or better!

4 have completed the course, you must write a report explaining the content of

4th –write report

the course and its relevance to your position. **Then**, you must fill out a reim-

5th –fill out reimb. request

5 + 6 bursement request. Attach a tuition payment receipt, your report, and a copy of

6th –attach tuition, report + grades to request

7 your grades to this request and **promptly** submit this request to your supervi-

sor. **Once** your supervisor has approved the request, you can **then** submit all of

7th –submit to supervisor

8 these forms to Human Resources, and you should receive your check within two

8th –submit to HR

weeks.

If you miss a step in this process, you won't be reimbursed. Thus, it's critical that you be able to identify each step and the order in which the steps must be taken.

SUMMARY

Chronological structure is, of course, a very useful organizational pattern. Events happen in a certain order, so writers often present them in that order. Keep an eye out for the transitional words and phrases that signal this type of organization.

Skill Building Until Next Time

- As you think about things today, try to organize them chronologically. If you think back to something that happened to you over the weekend, for example, think about it in the order it happened: First I _____, then _____, suddenly, _____, and so on.
- As you read about events in the newspaper or in other places, put the different pieces of each event in chronological order, as you did with the story about Mr. Blank.

L·E·S·S·O·N
ORDER OF IMPORTANCE

7

LESSON SUMMARY

Continuing your study of the structure of reading material, this lesson shows you how writers use order of importance—from least to most important or from most to least important. Understanding this commonly used structure improves your reading comprehension by helping you see what's most important in a piece of writing.

t's a scientifically proven fact: People remember most what they learn *first* and *last* in a given session. Writers have instinctively known this for a long time. That's why many pieces of writing are organized not in chronological order but *by order of importance*.

Imagine again that the writer is like an architect. How would this type of writer arrange the rooms? By hierarchy. A *hierarchy* is a group of things arranged by rank or order of importance. In this type of organizational pattern, *hierarchy*, not chronology, determines order. Thus, this architect would lay the rooms out like so: When you walk in the front door, the first room you encounter would be the president's office, then the vice president's, then the assistant vice president's, and so on down to the lowest ranking worker. Or, vice versa, the architect may choose for you to meet the least important employee first, the one who has the least power in the company. Then the next, and the next, until at last you reach the president.

Likewise, in writing, ideas may be arranged in order of importance. In this pattern, which idea comes first? Not the one that *happened* first, but the one that is *most*, or *least*, important.

MOST IMPORTANT TO LEAST IMPORTANT

In the following paragraph, the writer starts with what is most important, hoping that by putting this item first, the reader will be sure to remember it. After you read the passage, answer the questions that follow. Each question is followed by its answer to guide you through your reading of the passage.

There are many things you can do to make tax time easier. The single most important thing you can do is to keep accurate records. Keep all of your pay stubs, receipts, bank statements, and so forth in a neat, organized folder so that when you're ready to prepare your form, all of your paperwork is in one place. The second thing you can do is start early. Get your tax forms from the post office as soon as they are available and start calculating. This way, if you run into any problems, you have plenty of time to straighten them out. You can also save time by reading the directions carefully. This will prevent time-consuming errors. Finally, if your taxes are relatively simple (you don't have any itemized deductions or special investments), use the shorter tax form. It's only one page, and if your records are in order, it can be completed in an hour or less.

1. According to the passage, what's the most important thing you can do to make tax time easier?

The answer, of course, should be clear: the writer tells you clearly that the "single most important thing" is to "keep accurate records."

2. What is the second most important thing you can do to make tax time easier?

When a writer starts out by saying "the most important thing," you know that the writer will be starting with the most important idea and ending with the least important. The second best thing, therefore, is the second piece of advice offered in the paragraph: "start early."

3. What's the third most important thing?

Did you write "Read the directions carefully"? Good.

4. Finally, what is the *least* important tip the writer offers?

Of course, the answer is the last piece of advice the writer offers: Use the short form if you can.

LEAST IMPORTANT TO MOST IMPORTANT

Some writers prefer the opposite approach, depending on the subject and the effect they want their writing to have. Rather than *starting* with the most important idea, they prefer to *end* with what is most important. Not only do they leave you with a strong concluding impression, but they also take advantage of the "snowball effect." The snowball effect is the "build up" or force that a writer gets from starting with what's least important and moving toward what's most important. Like a snowball, the writer's idea builds and builds, gets bigger and bigger, more and more important. By starting with the least important point, writers can also create suspense—the reader is waiting for that final idea. And each idea or item builds upon the ones that come before it (as in a snowball).

Here's an example of a paragraph that builds from least important to most important. Read the paragraph, marking it up as you go along. Answer the questions that follow.

There are a number of reasons why there should not be dress-down days at work. First of all, workplaces need to maintain a conscious distinction between the professional and the casual. This distinction is maintained largely by dress. When this distinction vanishes, workers might begin to be more casual with each other, making it difficult to maintain a professional atmosphere.

More importantly, casual wear destroys company hierarchy. When the president of the company comes to work wearing khaki pants and a polo shirt, employees are likely to say, "Why, he's just one of us." While in "real life" he may indeed be their equal, in the workplace he is not.

But the most important reason employees should not be allowed to come to work dressed casually is because it drastically decreases productivity. When people are dressed in their work clothes, they work; when they are dressed casually, the temptation to be casual about getting work done is too great. Employees spend a great deal of time milling about and have a great tendency to cut corners: "Oh, I don't need to proofread this again. It's good enough." This attitude in the workplace can not only be dangerous to a company's welfare—it can be deadly.

In the spaces below, first list the reasons the author provides for being against dressing casually at work *in the order in which they are listed in the passage.* In the next set of blanks, list those same reasons *in their order of importance.*

Order of Presentation

1.

2.

3.

Order of Importance

1.

2.

3.

You see, of course, that the orders are reversed: The author starts with what is least important and ends with what is most important. Why? Why not the other way around?

This author uses a least-to-most-important organizational strategy because he is making an argument. He's trying to convince you that it's not a good idea to have dress-down days at work. In order to be convincing, he must have a pretty strong argument. If he starts with what he feels is his most important (and most convincing) point, he has already shown his hand, so to speak. And he hasn't "warmed you up" yet. Especially when the issue is controversial, writers often use the least-to-most-important structure. That way, if their less important points make sense to the reader, then their more important points will come off even stronger. Also, if they were to organize their ideas in the reverse order, most to least important, readers might feel let down.

Thus, you can often expect to see this type of structure—least to most important—in an argument. As the saying goes, "save the best for last." In an argument, that's usually where "the best" has the most impact.

In the first example, about preparing for tax time, the writer was not trying to convince. She was simply giving some advice. There's no need, then, for a build-up. Indeed, in that kind of paragraph, the reader might stop reading after the first tip if he or she doesn't find it helpful. That's why the most important ideas come first—to make sure they'll be read.

In other words, the writer's *purpose*, his or her motive for writing, influences the choice of organizational patterns. In turn, the structure influences how you take in and understand what you read.

PRACTICE

Look at the following list of reasons to read more often. If you were to put these reasons together in a paragraph to convince readers that they should read more, how would you organize them? Rank these reasons first in order of importance and then in the order in which you would present them.

Five Reasons to Read More Often

- It will improve your vocabulary.
- It will improve your reading comprehension.
- It will increase your reading speed.
- It will broaden your understanding of yourself and others.
- It will introduce you to new information and ideas.

Order of Importance to You

1.

2.

3.

4.

5.

Order of Presentation

1.

2.

3.

4.

5.

In which order did you choose to present your ideas? Most important to least important? Or least to most? Either structure will work beautifully with these ideas. You may want to hit your readers with what's most important from the start so that you make sure you catch their attention. Or you may want to save your best idea for last so that your readers get through all the other ideas first and build up to the most important. You might present the ideas differently, but below are two versions of the resulting paragraph as examples.

Example: Most to Least Important

There are many benefits to reading more often. First and foremost, reading more will broaden your understanding of yourself and of other people. It will also introduce you to new information and ideas. Furthermore, it will improve your overall reading comprehension so you'll begin to understand more of what you read. In addition, reading more will improve your vocabulary and increase your reading speed.

Example: Least to Most Important

There are many benefits to reading more often. First of all, it will increase your reading speed, so that you can read more in less time. Second, it will improve your vocabulary. Third, it will improve your overall reading comprehension, and you'll understand more of what you read. In addition, reading more will introduce you to new information and ideas. Most importantly, it will broaden your understanding of yourself and of other people.

REVIEW
Transitions

Notice how the transitional words and phrases are used in the paragraphs above. Go back to each paragraph and underline the transitional words and phrases.

Here are the words you should have underlined in the first paragraph: *first and foremost, also, furthermore, in addition.* The second paragraph uses different transitional words and phrases: *first of all, second, third, in addition,* and *most importantly.*

Main Idea

By the way, what is the main idea of the two paragraphs above? Do you see a topic sentence? Write the main idea of the paragraphs in the space below.

You can probably recognize by now that the first sentence in each paragraph, "There are many benefits to reading more often," is the topic sentence that governs each paragraph. This sentence is general enough to encompass each of the different reasons given, and it makes an assertion about reading—that you should do it more often.

SUMMARY

Organizing ideas by order of importance is a structure you will see often. Whether a passage is organized from most to least important or least to most, this technique should now be easy for you to recognize.

Skill Building Until Next Time

- As you come across lists today, see how they are organized. Are they organized by order of importance? If so, are the items listed from least to most important or from most to least? If the lists are not organized hierarchically, try to organize them by their order of importance.
- Create your own "order of importance" paragraphs like the one on reasons to read more often. Some topics you might write about are reasons why you shouldn't have to take a certain required course, reasons why your college should sponsor more social events, things you want to accomplish before you graduate, and so forth.

L·E·S·S·O·N

SIMILARITIES AND DIFFERENCES: COMPARE AND CONTRAST

8

LESSON SUMMARY

Today's lesson explores another organizational pattern writers often use to structure their writing: comparison and contrast.

W
e spend a good deal of our lives comparing and contrasting things. Whenever we want to explain something, for example, we often use *comparison* (showing how two or more things are *similar*). We might say, for example, that mint chocolate chip ice cream tastes just like a York Peppermint Pattie; or that the new professor looks just like Clint Eastwood. When we want to show how things are *different* or not alike, we *contrast* them. We might say that York Peppermint Patties are mintier than any mint chocolate chip ice cream; or that the new professor may look like Eastwood, but he doesn't have Eastwood's dimple.

How Comparison and Contrast Work

What writers do when they compare and contrast is provide a way of classifying or judging the items they're analyzing. They show how two (or more) things are similar or different when placed side by side. Consider, for example, the following paragraph. Read it carefully and then answer the questions that follow. The answers are after the questions.

Being a secretary is a lot like being a parent. After a while, your boss becomes dependent on you, just as a child is dependent on his or her mother or father. Like a child who must ask permission before going out, you'll find your boss coming to you for permission, too. "Can I have a meeting on Tuesday at 3:30?" you might be asked, because you're the one who keeps track of your boss's schedule. You will also find yourself cleaning up after your boss a lot, especially at the end of the day, putting papers away in the same way a parent tucks away toys and clothes. A parent protects his or her children from outside dangers; likewise, you too will find yourself protecting your boss from certain "dangers"—unwanted callers, angry clients, upset subordinates. However, a parent's responsibility for his or her child lessens with the years as the child learns to do more and more on his or her own. A secretary's responsibilities for his or her boss only grow more and more with each year.

FINDING THE FACTS

1. What two things are being compared and contrasted here?

2. In what ways are these two things similar? (There are four similarities; list them below.)

a.

b.

c.

d.

3. In what ways are these two things different? (There is one aspect that is different; write it below.)

Answers

1. The two things being compared and contrasted are a parent and a secretary.

2. Secretaries are like parents in that: a) bosses are dependent on secretaries as children are on parents; b) bosses seek permission from their secretaries as children do from their parents; c) secretaries clean up after their bosses, as parents do after children; and d) secretaries protect their bosses, as parents protect their children.

3. Secretaries are unlike parents in that their responsibility for their boss grows instead of lessens with the years.

FINDING THE MAIN IDEA

Now that you've answered those questions, consider one more. Look at the passage above again, and then answer this question:

4. What is the main idea of this passage?

Did you notice that the opening sentence, "Being a secretary is a lot like being a parent," is the topic sentence that expresses the main idea of this paragraph? The paragraph does mention a *difference* between these two roles, but notice that the topic sentence does not claim that secretaries and parents are *exactly* alike. Instead, it asserts that they are "a lot" alike.

TRANSITIONAL DEVICES

As you read the paragraph about secretaries and mothers, did you notice the transitional words and phrases that show you when the writer is comparing (showing similarity) and when the writer is contrasting (showing difference)? Here's the passage once more. As you read it this time, underline the transitional words and phrases you find.

Being a secretary is a lot like being a parent. After a while, your boss becomes dependent on you, just as a child is dependent on his or her mother or father. Like a child who must ask permission before going out, you'll find your boss coming to you for permission, too. "Can I have a meeting on Tuesday at 3:30?" you might be asked, because you're the one who keeps track of your boss's schedule. You will also find yourself cleaning up after your boss a lot, especially at the end of the day, putting papers away in the same way a parent tucks away toys and clothes. A parent protects his or her children from outside dangers; likewise, you too will find yourself protecting your boss from certain "dangers"—unwanted callers, angry clients, upset subordinates. However, a parent's responsibility for his or her child lessens with the years as the child learns to do more and more on his or her own. A secretary's responsibilities for his or her boss only grow more and more with each year.

There are several transitional words and phrases writers use to show comparison and contrast. In this paragraph, you should have underlined the following words: *just as, like, in the same way, likewise,* and *however.* Below is a more complete list of transitional words and phrases.

Here are some words and phrases that show similarity:

similarly	in the same way
likewise	in a like manner
like	and
just as	also

These are words and phrases that show difference:

but	yet
on the other hand	on the contrary
however	nevertheless
conversely	

STRUCTURE

Now look more closely at the sample paragraph to examine its structure. Exactly how is this paragraph organized?

First, you've noticed that the paragraph begins with a topic sentence that makes the initial comparison:

secretaries are like parents. Then, the paragraph identifies four ways in which secretaries are like parents:

1. Bosses become dependent upon secretaries as children do on parents.

2. Bosses seek permission from their secretaries as children do from parents.

3. Secretaries clean up after their bosses as parents do after children.

4. Secretaries protect bosses from "dangers" as parents protect children.

Finally, after pointing out these similarities, the paragraph concludes by pointing out an important difference between parents and secretaries:

1. A secretary's responsibility for his or her boss increases with time while a parent's lessens.

Perhaps you noticed something else in the way this paragraph is organized. Did you notice that every time the paragraph mentions something about a parent's role, it also mentions something about a secretary? Each aspect of the parent's role that is discussed is followed by a comparable aspect of the secretary's role. Thus, for every aspect of "A" (the parent), the paragraph provides a comparable aspect of "B" (the secretary) to compare or contrast. The paragraph is therefore organized like this: ABABABABAB.

This is called the **point-by-point** method of comparison and contrast. Each aspect of A that is discussed is immediately paired with that aspect of B (being dependent, getting permission, cleaning up, protecting, and dependence).

On the other hand, some writers prefer to deal first with all aspects of A and then with all aspects of B. This is called the **block** method of comparison and contrast;

it goes AAAAABBBBB. Here is the same paragraph arranged using the block method:

Being a secretary is a lot like being a parent. Children are dependent on their parents, and they must seek permission from their parents to do certain things. Parents spend a lot of time cleaning up after their children, particularly putting away toys and clothes. And parents also protect their children from outside dangers. A parent's responsibility for his or her child, however, lessens with time as the child becomes more independent.

Like parents, secretaries often find their bosses become dependent on them. Like children, bosses come to their secretary for permission for certain things. "Can I have a meeting on Tuesday at 3:30?" a boss might ask, because the secretary keeps the boss's schedule. Secretaries also find themselves cleaning up after their bosses at the end of the day. Like parents, secretaries also often protect their bosses from outside "dangers" such as unwanted callers, angry clients, and upset subordinates. However, unlike parents, secretaries will find that their responsibility for their boss grows more and more each year.

Here, the passage treats each of the things being compared and contrasted separately—first, all aspects of the parent, then all aspects of the secretary—rather than one aspect of the parent, one of the secretary; another of the parent, another of the secretary. So the organization is quite different.

But you should notice one thing that is the same in both passages: They compare and contrast aspects of A and B that are comparable or parallel. When an aspect of A is discussed, that same aspect of B (whether it is similar to or different from A's) must be discussed. This correspondence of parts is essential for the compare and contrast technique. Look what happens, for example, when the writer does not discuss corresponding parts:

Being a secretary is a lot like being a parent. Parents must bathe, clothe, and feed their children. Parents must also create and maintain guidelines for acceptable behavior for children. And parents must see to it that their children get a proper education.

Secretaries manage their boss's schedule and files. They will often make travel and meeting arrangements for their boss as well. And secretaries will often serve as a protective barrier between their boss and other people.

You'll notice that this passage seems to focus on differences between parents and secretaries rather than the similarities. But is this really a fair contrast? Look at the aspects of A (the parent) that are described here. Do they have any relationship to the aspects of B (the secretary) that are described? No. And a compare and contrast passage can't be successful unless the aspects of A and B discussed are comparable. The two paragraphs above don't really seem to have a point—there's no basis for comparison between parents and secretaries.

PRACTICE

Suppose you were going to write a paragraph that compares and contrasts readers and detectives. There are five aspects of being a reader and five aspects of being a detective listed below. Only *three* items in each list are comparable. Find those three items in each list and pair connecting them with their matching item. Remember, these items may be either similarities or differences. What's important is that they are comparable aspects.

A reader:

1. Looks for clues to meaning.

2. Has many different types of books to read.

3. Can choose what book to read.

4. Builds vocabulary by reading.

5. Becomes a better reader with each book.

A detective:

1. Has a dangerous job.

2. Gets better at solving crimes with each case.

3. Requires lots of training.

4. Doesn't get to choose which cases to work on.

5. Looks for clues to solve the crime.

Did you find the aspects that are comparable? Did you match Reader 1 with Detective 5 (similarity)? Reader 3 with Detective 4 (difference)? And Reader 5 with Detective 2 (similarity)? If so, you did terrific work.

Here's how this information might work together in a paragraph:

In many ways, readers are a lot like detectives. Like detectives looking for clues at the scene of the crime, readers look for clues to meaning in the books that they read. And, like detectives who get better and better at solving crimes with each case, readers get better and better at understanding what they read with each book. Unfortunately for detectives, however, they cannot choose which cases they get to work on, whereas readers have the pleasure of choosing which books they'd like to read.

WHY COMPARE AND CONTRAST?

In addition to following the ABABAB or AAABBB structure, compare and contrast passages must, like all other passages, have a point. There's a reason that these two items are being compared and contrasted; there's something the writer is trying to point out by putting these two things side by side for analysis. This reason or point is the main idea, which is often stated in a topic sentence.

The main idea of the first paragraph you looked at today was "Being a secretary is a lot like being a parent." In this paragraph, you learned that the writer sees a significant similarity between these two roles. Likewise, in the paragraph above, you see a significant similarity between readers and detectives.

In both cases, you may never have thought of making such comparisons. That's part of the beauty of the compare and contrast organization: It often allows you to see things in a new and interesting way. In addition, it serves the more practical function of showing you how two things measure up against each other so that you can make informed decisions, like about which car to buy (a compare and contrast essay might tell you which car is better) or which savings bond to invest in (a compare and contrast essay will show you which bond is best for you).

Skill Building Until Next Time

- As you go through your day, compare and contrast things around you. Compare and contrast, for example, your English class to your math class. How are they alike? How are they different? Make sure the aspects of the two classes that you analyze are comparable. For example, you might want to compare and contrast the work load, professor's teaching style, and type of discussion in both classes.

- As you make these comparisons, or if you notice compare and contrast passages in what you read, practice arranging them in both point-by-point order (ABABAB) and in block order (AAABBB).

L·E·S·S·O·N 9

WHY DO THINGS HAPPEN? A LOOK AT CAUSE AND EFFECT

LESSON SUMMARY

"One thing leads to another"—that's the principle behind cause and effect. Understanding cause and effect, and the relationship between them, will make you a better reader.

F or every action," the famous scientist Sir Isaac Newton said, "there is an equal and opposite reaction." Every action results in another action (a *reaction*); or, for every action, there is an *effect* caused by that action. Likewise, each action is *caused* by a previous action. In other words, each action has a *cause*—something that made it happen— and each action has an *effect*—something it makes happen.

- **Cause:** a person or thing that makes something happen or produces an effect.
- **Effect:** a change produced by an action or cause.

Much of what you read is an attempt to explain either the cause of some action or its effect. For example, an author might try to explain the causes of World War I or the effect of underwater nuclear testing; the reason behind a change in course requirements for math majors or the effect budget cuts will have on school-sponsored social events. Let's take a look at how writers explaining cause or effect might organize their ideas.

DISTINGUISHING CAUSE FROM EFFECT

A passage that examines cause generally answers the question *why* something took place: Why was funding for language clubs cut? Who or what made this take place? A passage that examines effect generally answers the question *what happened* after something took place: What happened as a result of the funding cut? How did it affect the language students?

PRACTICE

To help you distinguish between cause and effect, look carefully at the sentences below. You'll see that cause and effect work together; you can't have one without the other. That's why it's very important to be able to distinguish between the two. See if you can determine both the cause and the effect in each of the following sentences:

Example: Robin got ten points off when he handed in his paper late.
Cause: Robin handed in his paper late.
Effect: Robin got ten points off.

1. Inflation has caused tuition to increase.
   Cause:

   Effect:

2. Since we hired new cooks, cafeteria food has been splendid.
   Cause:

   Effect:

3. He realized that his car had stopped not because it needed repair but because it ran out of gas.
   Cause:

   Effect:

4. The university's budget crisis was created by overspending.
   Cause:

   Effect:

5. As a result of our new registration process, students are much happier.
   Cause:

   Effect:

Answers

1. **Cause:** *Inflation*
   Effect: *Tuition was increased.*
2. **Cause:** *We hired new cooks.*
   Effect: *Cafeteria food has been splendid.*
3. **Cause:** *The car ran out of gas.*
   Effect: *The car stopped.*
4. **Cause:** *Overspending*
   Effect: *Budget crisis*
5. **Cause:** *The new registration process*
   Effect: *Students have been happier.*

You were probably guided in your answers to the exercise above by the words and phrases that indicate when a cause or effect is being examined. Below is a partial list of such words.

Words Indicating Cause

because (of)	created (by)
since	caused (by)

Words Indicating Effect

since	therefore
hence	consequently
so	as a result

WHEN CAUSE AND EFFECT ARE INTERRELATED

Notice how the signal words listed on the previous page are used in the following paragraph. Underline the signal words as you come across them.

Ed became a mechanic largely because of his father. His father was always in the garage working on one car or another, so young Ed would spend hours watching his father work. As a result, he became fascinated by cars at an early age. His father encouraged him to learn about cars on his own, so Ed began tinkering with cars himself at age eight. Consequently, by the time he was 13, Ed could tear an engine apart and put it back together by himself. Since he was already so skilled, when he was 15 he got a job as the chief mechanic at a local repair shop. He has been there ever since.

You should have underlined the following signal words and phrases in the paragraph above: *because of*, *so* (twice), *as a result*, *consequently*, and *since*.

Notice that this paragraph's purpose—to explain *why* Ed became a mechanic—is expressed in the topic sentence, "Ed became a mechanic largely because of his father." This paragraph's purpose, then, is to explain cause, and the primary cause is Ed's father.

You'll notice, however, that some of the sentences in this paragraph also deal with effect. This may seem like a contradiction at first. After all, why would a paragraph about cause deal with effect? But it's not a contradiction. That's because there isn't just *one* thing that led to Ed's becoming a mechanic. Although Ed's dad may have been the initial cause, there was still a *series* of actions and reactions that took place—a series of causes and effects. Once A causes B, B then becomes the cause for C.

In fact, there are six different sets of cause and effect listed in this paragraph. What are they? The first cause is provided to get you started.

Cause 1: Ed's father was always in the garage.

Effect 1:

Cause 2:

Effect 2:

Cause 3:

Effect 3:

Cause 4:

Effect 4:

Cause 5:

Effect 5:

Cause 6:

Effect 6:

Answers

Cause 1: Ed's father was always in the garage.
Effect 1: Ed would spend hours watching.

Cause 2: Ed would spend hours watching.
Effect 2: Ed became fascinated by cars.

Cause 3: Ed became fascinated by cars.
Effect 3: Ed began tinkering with cars.

Cause 4: Ed began tinkering with cars.
Effect 4: Ed's father encouraged him.

Cause 5: Ed's father encouraged him.
Effect 5: Ed could tear an engine apart by himself.

Cause 6: Ed could tear an engine apart by himself.
Effect 6: He got a job as the chief mechanic.

VARIATIONS

WHEN ONE CAUSE HAS SEVERAL EFFECTS

Sometimes one cause may have several effects: Several things may happen as a result of one action. In the passage below, the writer explains several effects of the new marketing campaign:

> Our new marketing campaign has been a tremendous success. Since we've been advertising on the radio, sales have increased by 35 percent. Our client references have doubled, and we've had greater client retention rates. Furthermore, we've been able to hire five new sales representatives and expand our territory to include the southwestern United States.

According to the paragraph above, what have been the effects of the new marketing campaign?

1.

2.

3.

4.

5.

Answers

1. Sales have increased 35 percent.
2. Client references have doubled.
3. Client retention rates have increased.
4. Five new sales representatives have been hired.
5. Territory has been expanded to include the Southwest.

WHEN ONE EFFECT HAS SEVERAL CAUSES

Just as one action can have many results, one action can have many causes as well. The following memo is an example.

> TO: Joe Smith
> FROM: Management
>
> This memorandum is to clarify the circumstances of your dismissal. Although you may think we've dismissed you because of your recent absenteeism, there are, in fact, several reasons behind our decision to terminate you. In addition to your excessive absence, you have failed to complete your monthly and weekly reports in a timely manner. In fact, many times we've received them so late that we were unable to include your figures in our budget reports. Furthermore, we have had several complaints recently regarding your conduct in the office, and several supervisors have reported your refusal to follow our company dress code. While none of these offenses would be worthy of dismissal on an individual basis,

combined they leave us no choice but to terminate your employment.

Why did Joe Smith get fired? List the causes below:

1.

2.

3.

4.

Answers

You should have noticed that there were four causes:

1. Joe's excessive absenteeism.
2. Joe's late reports.
3. Complaints about Joe's conduct.
4. Joe's refusal to follow the dress code.

CONTRIBUTING VS. SUFFICIENT CAUSE

You'll notice that the memorandum above tells Mr. Smith that "none of these offenses would be worthy of dismissal on an individual basis." This means that each of these causes is a **contributing** cause. A *contributing* cause is one that *helps* to make something happen but can't make that thing happen by itself. It is only one factor that *contributes* to the cause.

On the opposite end of the cause spectrum is the **sufficient** cause. A *sufficient* cause is an event that, by itself, is strong enough to make the event happen. Sufficient cause is demonstrated in the following paragraph.

Dear Mr. X:

We have recently learned that you have breached our Confidentiality Agreement. When you joined our company, you agreed not to reveal any of our company secrets to the competition. You also agreed that if you were found in violation of this agreement, your employment would be terminated. Consequently, we hereby terminate your employment, effective immediately. Please see Myra in Payroll for your final paycheck.

Here, you can see that there is one clear reason why Mr. X is being fired: He breached the Confidentiality Agreement. (If you don't know what *breach* means, you should be able to determine the meaning from the context.)

EVALUATING OPINIONS ABOUT CAUSE AND EFFECT

Sometimes in a cause and effect passage, an author will offer his or her *opinion* about the cause or effect of something rather than *facts* about the cause or effect. In that case, readers must judge the validity of the author's analysis. Are the author's ideas logical? Does he or she support the conclusions he or she comes to? Consider, for example, two authors' opinions about how a no-smoking policy would affect their office.

Paragraph A

A no-smoking policy would be disastrous. Over one-third of our employees smoke an average of three-quarters of a pack each per day. Since they will no longer be allowed to smoke in the office, they will need to take longer breaks (since they must now leave the building in order to smoke). As a result, they will be less productive. In addition, because their breaks must be longer, they must take fewer breaks and only at certain times in the day when they are able to get away for longer periods of time. Consequently, there will be long stretches of time between cigarettes for them, so many of these employees will be extremely irritable. This irritability will inevitably affect their coworkers. Furthermore, many long-term smokers will simply quit their jobs rather than put up with this irritability. They will simply find another company that will let them smoke at work.

Paragraph B

A no-smoking policy will be a tremendous benefit to all of our employees. If smoking is eliminated in the office, all employees will be able to breathe air free from any second-hand smoke while at work. Furthermore, our clean air won't drive out any potential clients or employees who are irritated by smoke. In addition, those who do smoke may find it easier to quit or at least reduce the number of cigarettes they smoke during the day because cigarette breaks will not be as accessible. Also, employees will be more productive since they won't be able to take such frequent cigarette breaks. Finally, we will be able to reduce the cost of our health-care benefits once our office officially becomes a no-smoking environment. This will save every employee money.

What effects does Author A think a no-smoking policy would have?

1.

2.

3.

4.

5.

What effects does Author B think a no-smoking policy would have?

1.

2.

3.

4.

5.

You'll notice that both authors take one cause—a no-smoking policy—and offer several possible effects. Often, authors will use the cause-and-effect structure to make arguments like the ones we've just seen: one for and one against a no-smoking policy. It is up to the reader to determine whose argument seems most valid.

SUMMARY

Understanding cause and effect is an important skill not only for reading comprehension but also for your daily life. In order to analyze the events happening around you, you have to be able to understand *why* those events happened—what caused them. Similarly, in order to make decisions or evaluate the decisions of others, you need to be able to think about the effects of a possible decision. "Reading," not only texts but also events and situations, requires you to understand cause and effect.

Skill Building Until Next Time

- As you go through your day or campus, think about how things have changed since before you were a college student. Perhaps now you can sleep later than you used to, you spend more time in the library, or maybe your entire outlook on life is different. These various changes are all effects of one large change—beginning school. Make a long list of all the effects you are experiencing. Then forecast the effect of changes that are coming. For example, how will graduation affect your life?
- Consider recent events at school or work. What might have caused them? For example, if a coworker just got a promotion, consider what he or she might have done to deserve that promotion. Or if the person you sit next to in math keeps getting F's on tests, what might be causing that trouble?

L·E·S·S·O·N

BEING STRUCTURALLY SOUND: PUTTING IT ALL TOGETHER

10

LESSON SUMMARY

Today's lesson pulls together what you've learned in Lessons 6–9 and gives you more practice in discerning the structure of a reading passage.

Like an architect designing a building, a writer must have a blueprint—a plan for how he or she will organize the passage. So far in this section we've looked at several ways that authors may organize their information and ideas:

- **Lesson 6: Chronological order.** Ideas are arranged in the order in which they occurred (or in the order in which they should occur).
- **Lesson 7: Order of importance.** Ideas are arranged in order of *increasing* importance (least important idea to most important idea) or in order of *decreasing* importance (most important idea to least important idea).
- **Lesson 8: Compare and contrast.** Ideas are arranged so that parallel aspects of item A and item B are compared and contrasted either in block style (AAAABBBB) or point-by-point style (ABABABAB).
- **Lesson 9: Cause and effect.** Ideas are arranged so that readers can see what event or series of events *caused* something to take place or what *effect* an event or series of events had.

If any of the terms or strategies on the previous page seem unfamiliar to you, STOP. Please take a few moments to review whatever lesson is unclear.

PRACTICE

Although writers often rely on one particular structure to organize their ideas, in many cases, writers use a combination of these structures. For example, a writer may want to compare and contrast the causes of World War I and those of World War II; or a writer may want to describe, in chronological order, the events that led to (caused) the failure of the computer system. Thus,

today we will look at how writers may combine these strategies. In addition, we'll continue to strengthen your reading comprehension skills by including strategies from the first week:

- Finding the facts
- Determining the main idea
- Defining vocabulary words in context
- Distinguishing between fact and opinion

PRACTICE PASSAGE 1

Begin with the following paragraph. Read it carefully, marking it up as you go. Then answer the questions that follow.

There are several reasons behind our decision to close the Florida office. The first difficulty occurred last May, when our long-time manager, John Doe, resigned. Although he left the company for purely personal reasons, and although sales were at their highest in months, many employees saw his departure as a symptom that the company was in trouble, and within a week after Mr. Doe's departure, several other employees quit. We were unable to fill Mr. Doe's position for some time, since all the candidates we interviewed were either discouraged by the number of employee vacancies or didn't have the experience to handle the work. Then the sales dropped dramatically, and, as a result, the office was unable to meet its monthly expenses. At the same time, our central office tightened its budget, so we lacked sufficient funds to revitalize the office. After a board meeting in August, we decided to close the office permanently. We will, of course, help relocate employees who wish to stay with the firm.

1. Which two organizational strategies does this writer use?
   a. chronological order
   b. order of importance
   c. compare and contrast
   d. cause and effect

2. *Revitalize* means
   a. to be very important, vital
   b. to relocate
   c. to bring back to life

3. What started the trouble in the Florida office?

4. What happened after the initial cause set things in motion?

a.

b.

c.

d.

e.

f.

Answers

1. a, d. The writer tells you the causes, in the order in which they occurred, that resulted in the closing of the Florida office.

2. c. You can tell from the context of the surrounding sentences that the company could not invest money in the office, and therefore the office had to be closed. If they could have invested money in the office, it is likely that they would have been able to bring the dying office back to life.

3. John Doe's resignation started the trouble in the Florida office.

4. After John Doe resigned, the following events occurred in this order:

a. The other employees quit.

b. They were unable to fill John Doe's position.

c. Sales dropped.

d. The office was unable to meet its expenses.

e. The central office tightened its budget.

f. They decided to close the office.

How did you do? Were you able to see how each cause led to an effect, and how that effect caused something else to happen (another effect)? If you missed any of the questions, here's what you should do:

If you missed:	Then study:
Question 1	Lessons 6 and 9
Question 2	Lesson 3
Question 3	Lesson 9
Question 4	Lesson 9

PRACTICE PASSAGE 2

Now try the passage on the next page. Again, read it carefully, marking it up as you go, and then answer the questions that follow.

There are several changes in the procedure for employees who wish to apply for vacant positions within the company. These changes make it much easier for in-house employees to fill vacancies that occur within the company.

First, the most important difference is that employees will now be notified of all available positions *before* the positions are advertised for the general public. Accordingly, all in-house candidates will be interviewed before we see any outside candidates, and we will offer the job to outside candidates only if no current employees are able to fill the position only.

Second, under the new procedure in-house employees can be hired even if they don't meet all job requirements. Under our old policy, in-house employees had to meet all job qualifications in order to obtain the vacant position. Now, however, employees who have proven themselves dedicated to the company will be hired for a vacant position even if they are lacking some minor qualifications; training will be provided.

A third change involves recommendations. From now on, employees do not need to be recommended for an in-house position before they apply. Instead, employees may apply as soon as they are aware of the vacancy. The remaining procedures and policies (those regarding increase in pay, interview procedure, and hiring approval) remain the same.

5. Which two organizational strategies does this writer use?
 a. chronological order
 b. order of importance
 c. compare and contrast
 d. cause and effect

6. The author organizes his ideas in order of
 a. decreasing importance (most important to least important)
 b. increasing importance (least important to most important)

7. Underline the sentence in this passage that expresses the main idea.

8. The sentence you underlined is
 a. fact
 b. opinion

Answers
5. b, c. The author uses order of importance in comparing the old procedure to the new one.
6. a. The author organizes his ideas in order of decreasing importance. He starts with the most important change ("First, the most important difference is . . .") and moves downward to the second and third most important changes.

7. The sentence that expresses the main idea of all four paragraphs is the second sentence in the first paragraph: "These changes make it much easier for in-house employees to fill vacancies." Although the first sentence tells us what all the paragraphs will be about (the changes in the procedure), it is the second sentence that expresses an opinion—how the author feels about this subject—and therefore it is the main idea.

8. b. This sentence expresses an opinion, not a fact. There have indeed been changes—that is a fact—but whether those changes make things easier for most employees is debatable. There may be some things about the old procedure that we don't know. Perhaps, for example, they opened the job to both in-house employees and the general public at the same time, but they interviewed all in-house employees first anyway. Because of our limited information about the old procedure, we cannot accept the idea that the change is better as fact.

If you missed some of these questions, now it's up to you to figure out which lessons to review

PRACTICE PASSAGE 3

Now it's your turn. In this exercise, you'll take a paragraph that is organized one way—by cause and effect—and add another structure: order of importance.

Here's what you should do: Re-read the two passages about the effect of a no-smoking policy. Decide which author you agree with most. Then, look carefully at the effects the author predicts. Which effect do you think is most important? Which is least important? Rank these effects in order of importance. Then, decide whether you want to start with the most important idea and end with the least important, or, vice versa, start with the least important and end with the most important. Finally, put it all together in a paragraph in the space provided.

Paragraph A

A no-smoking policy would be disastrous. Over one-third of our employees smoke an average of three-quarters of a pack each per day. Since they will no longer be allowed to smoke in the office, they will need to take longer breaks (since they must now leave the building in order to smoke). As a result, they will be less productive. In addition, because their breaks must be longer, they must take fewer breaks and only at certain times in the day when they are able to get away for longer periods of time. Consequently, there will be long stretches of time between cigarettes for them, so many of these employees will be extremely irritable. This irritability will inevitably affect their coworkers. Furthermore, many long-term smokers will simply quit their jobs rather than put up with this irritability. They will simply find another company that will let them smoke at work.

Paragraph B

A no-smoking policy will be a tremendous benefit to all of our employees. If smoking is eliminated in the office, all employees will be able to breathe air free from any second-hand smoke while at work. Furthermore, our clean air won't drive out any potential clients or employees who are irritated by smoke. In addition, those who do smoke may find it easier to quit or at least reduce the number of cigarettes they smoke during the day because cigarette breaks will not be as accessible. Also, employees will be more productive since they won't be able to take such frequent cigarette breaks. Finally, we will be able to reduce the cost of our health-care benefits once our office officially becomes a no-smoking environment. This will save every employee money.

1. Rank the ideas of the paragraph you have chosen in order of their importance to you.

2. Now write a paragraph, choosing whether to put the ideas in the order of increasing importance or decreasing importance.

Skill Building Until Next Time

- Look again at the passages you read in Lessons 1–5. What structures do you notice at work in those paragraphs?
- As you read (and write) during the next few days, be aware of the structure of each paragraph you come across. Try to identify the author's strategy; try to use different strategies in your own writing.

LANGUAGE AND STYLE

In most of the passages you have read so far, the author's ideas and intentions have been very clear. But what happens when they're not? What if the writer doesn't provide a topic sentence that clearly expresses the main idea? Or what if the writer gives you a poem instead of a clear-cut memorandum? How do you figure out what the author is trying to say?

The good news is that no matter how cryptic a piece of writing may seem, the author always leaves clues to help you figure out what he or she means. These clues can be found in the writer's **language** and **style**—the words the writer uses and the type of sentences in which he or she uses them. The next four lessons, therefore, focus on four different aspects of language and style:

- Point of view
- Diction
- Style
- Tone

You'll learn how authors use these elements to create meaning for their readers. Then you'll put it all together in Lesson 15 to see how language, style, structure, and meaning work together.

A MATTER OF PERSPECTIVE: POINT OF VIEW

11

LESSON SUMMARY

This lesson introduces you to the concept of *point of view*, one strategy writers use to convey their meaning to readers. Aspects such as whether writers use the more subjective *I* or the more objective *one*, whether they address readers as *you* or merely refer to an anonymous *they*, influence how readers understand what the writer has written.

Picture this: You are walking along a tree-lined street late in the afternoon. Just ahead of you a woman is sitting on a bench; a dog lies in the shade at her feet. You watch them and nod hello as you walk by.

Now, picture this: You are that dog. You're sitting in the shade under a bench next to your owner's feet. Suddenly someone walks down the street in front of you. If you look up, you can see that person nod as he or she walks by.

Although you've just pictured the same thing—a person walking by a woman with a dog—you've really pictured two very different scenes, haven't you? The scenario looks quite different from the dog's point of view than from the walker's.

This shift in perspective happens in writing by changing the point of view. Point of view is one of the first choices writers make when they begin to write, because it is the point of view that determines who is speaking to the reader.

Point of view is the person or perspective through which the writer channels his or her information and ideas. Just as we may look at a physical object from a number of different perspectives (from above it, below it, behind it, beside it, and so on), we can look at information and ideas from different perspectives as well (mine, yours, his or hers, the professor's, the country's, and so on).

THREE KINDS OF POINT OF VIEW

When it comes to expressing point of view, writers can use three distinct approaches:

- **First person point of view** is a highly individualized, personal point of view in which the writer or narrator speaks about his or her own feelings and experiences directly to the reader using these pronouns: *I, me, mine; we, our, us.*
- **Second person point of view** is another personal point of view in which the writer speaks directly to the reader, addressing the reader as *you.*
- **Third person point of view** is an impersonal, objective point of view in which the perspective is that of an outsider (a "third person") who is not directly involved in the action. There is no direct reference to either the reader (second person) or the writer (first person). The writer chooses from these pronouns: *he, him, his; she, her, hers; it, its;* and *they, them, theirs.*

All of these points of view are available to writers, but not all of them may be appropriate for what they're writing, and only one of them will create the exact effect a writer desires. That's because each approach establishes a particular relationship between the reader and the writer.

WHEN WRITERS USE FIRST PERSON

Imagine you get one of the following messages from your company's head office:

A. The company congratulates you on the birth of your child.

B. We congratulate you on the birth of your child.

Which message would you rather receive?

Most of us would probably prefer to receive message B over message A. Why? What is the difference between these two messages? Both messages use the second person point of view, right? They both address the reader as "you." But you probably noticed that the writers chose different points of view to refer to themselves. Message A uses the third person point of view ("the company") whereas message B uses the first person pronoun "we." As a result, message B seems more sincere because it comes *from* a person *to* a person rather than from "the company" (a thing) to a person (*you*).

But the messages above do more than just express congratulations to the reader. They also seem to indicate something about how the people in the head office want to be perceived. In fact, their choice of point of view shows whether they want to be seen as people ("we") or as an entity ("the company"). Read the messages again and then decide how you think each writer wants to be perceived.

Which message seems to tell the reader, "We can speak directly to you because we are real people behind this company"?

Message _____

Which message seems to tell the reader, "We have a very formal relationship; let's not get too personal"?

Message _____

The company that sends message A suggests to the reader that "We have a very formal relationship; let's not get too close or too personal." Message B, on the other hand, tells the reader something more like this: "*We* can speak directly to *you* because we are real people behind this company." Thus, the point of view reflects the way the senders of the message wish to be perceived—as a distant entity (message A) or as friendly colleagues (message B).

DISTANCE VS. INTIMACY

Whether writers intend it or not (though they almost always do), the third person point of view establishes a certain distance between the writer and the reader. There's no direct person-to-person contact that way (*me* to *you*). Rather, with the third person point of view, someone (or something) else is speaking to the reader.

The first person point of view, on the other hand, establishes a certain intimacy between the writer and the reader. The writer uses *I, my, mine, we, our,* or *us* as if expressing his or her own personal feelings and ideas directly to the reader. "*We* congratulate you" makes message B much more personal than message A, where *the company* congratulates you.

- First person point of view establishes intimacy. The writer wants to be close to the reader.
- Third person point of view establishes distance. The writer wants to distance him- or herself from the reader.

WHEN WRITERS USE THIRD PERSON

In an academic environment, as in business, it's not always practical to be personal. Though the first person point of view may make the reader feel close to the writer,

the first person point of view also implies a certain *subjectivity*. That is, the writer is expressing a very personal view from a very personal perspective.

SUBJECTIVITY VS. OBJECTIVITY

There's nothing wrong with expressing personal views, but in college and in the business world, writers may not always be at an advantage using the first-person point of view. They're more likely to be taken seriously when they're *objective*, presenting things from an outsider's point of view, than when they're *subjective*, presenting things from their own possibly selfish or biased point of view.

- **Subjective**: based on the thoughts, feelings, and experiences of the speaker or writer (first person point of view)
- **Objective**: unaffected by the thoughts, feelings, and experiences of the speaker or writer (third person point of view)

Thus, if you wanted to complain about a new office policy, which of the following points of view do you think would be more effective?

A. I think our new office policy is a failure.

B. The new office policy appears to be a failure.

Most people would agree that sentence B is more effective. The question is, *why*?

1. The point of view of sentence B is more effective than that of sentence A because
   a. sentence A is too subjective
   b. sentence B is too subjective
   c. sentence A is too objective
   d. all of the above

The answer is **a.** Sentence A uses the first person point of view, and because *I* is so subjective and personal, it doesn't carry as much weight as the objective sentence B. In sentence B, there is no personal perspective; someone from the outside (a third person, not the reader or the writer) is looking at the policy and evaluating it. The third person point of view is almost always considered to be more objective because the third person is not directly involved in the action. *I*, however, *is* directly involved in the action (the policy) and therefore cannot have an objective opinion about the policy's success or failure. *I*'s opinion may be prejudiced by the writer's personal experience.

Of course, even when a writer uses third person, he or she can still express his or her own opinion. When that opinion is expressed in the third person, however, it *appears* much more objective.

WHEN WRITERS USE SECOND PERSON

When is *you* an appropriate pronoun? What effect does it create for you, the reader? *You* generally is used to address the reader directly, particularly when the writer is giving directions. Imagine, for example, that you have just started a new job. On your first day of work, you receive the following memo:

Memo A

As a new employee, you need to take care of several items in your first week of work. First, you need to visit our Human Resources Office to complete your new employee file. Second, you need to visit our Payroll Office to be added to our payroll. Finally, you need to meet with your immediate supervisor to develop your first six-month statement of goals.

Now, imagine you receive this memo instead:

Memo B

New employees must take care of several items during their first week of work. First, they must go

to the Human Resources Office to complete a new employee file. Second, they must go to the Payroll Office to be added to the payroll. Finally, they must meet with their immediate supervisor to develop their first six-month statement of goals.

Which memo would you rather receive? _____

Most likely you'd rather receive Memo A. Now, here's the tougher question:

2. The point of view of Memo A is more effective than the point of view of Memo B because
   a. Memo A feels less formal
   b. Memo A speaks personally to the reader
   c. Memo A addresses the reader as an individual
   d. all of the above

Most people would prefer Memo A for all of these reasons, so the answer is **d.** First of all, in Memo A, the writer speaks directly to the reader (*you*). In Memo B, the writer speaks in the third person ("new employees"); the memo never acknowledges that *you* are a new employee. As a result, Memo B sounds more formal or official. The second person point of view, however, addresses you personally. It also singles you out as an individual, not as a category (new employees). It is almost like Memo A was written just for you.

SECOND PERSON AND AUDIENCE

In fact, because Memo A uses the second person point of view, you can make certain assumptions about the audience for this memo. Re-read Memo A and then answer this question:

3. Memo A was most likely written for
   a. all employees
   b. managers of new employees
   c. new employees only
   d. Human Resources employees

Because Memo A uses the second person pronoun *you*, you can assume that it is being given **c**, *only* to new employees. It must be, because it can't work for any other audience because of its pronoun.

Memo B, on the other hand, could be used for a much larger audience. In fact, the memo could be part of a larger document addressed to all employees, or it could be directed to all the people mentioned in the paragraph (new employees, Human Resources, Payroll personnel, and supervisors). So the third person point of view may have been used in Memo B not to create a distance between the reader and the writer, but to allow for a wider audience.

Writers may also use *you* to make readers feel as if they are taking part in the action or ideas being expressed in the text. For example, let's imagine that a writer wants to convince readers that a four-day work week is a good idea. The writer could use the third person point of view as in the following paragraph:

Paragraph A

Imagine how wonderful it would be if employees had a four-day work week. Rather than working five eight-hour days (40 hours), employees would work four ten-hour days (still 40 hours). Then, they would have Friday, Saturday, and Sunday off. This would give employees a three-day weekend *every week*. The benefits of this extra day would be numerous. Employees would have a full day for running errands that can't be done while they're at work; a day to clean while their kids are at school so that they could have leisurely family weekends; one less day of child care expenses they would have to pay; an extra day of rest. Psychologically, employees would also benefit by feeling that there's almost a fair balance in their lives between work (four days) and rest (three days).

Or the writer could use the second person point of view to express the same ideas.

Paragraph B

Imagine how wonderful it would be if you had a four-day work week. Rather than working five eight-hour days (40 hours), you'd work four ten-hour days (still 40 hours). Then, you'd have Friday, Saturday, and Sunday off. This would give you a three-day weekend *every week*. The benefits of this extra day would be numerous. You'd have a full day for running errands that you can't get done while you're at work; a day to clean while your kids are at school so that you could have leisurely family weekends; one less day of child care expenses you'd have to pay; an extra day for you to rest. Psychologically, you would also benefit by feeling that there's almost a fair balance in your life between work (four days) and rest (three days).

Did you notice the difference between the paragraphs? What pronouns does each paragraph use?

4. Paragraph A uses
   a. first person pronouns (*I, we*)
   b. second person pronouns (*you*)
   c. third person pronouns (*he, she, they*)

5. Paragraph B uses
   a. first person pronouns (*I, we*)
   b. second person pronouns (*you*)
   c. third person pronouns (*he, she, they*)

Paragraph A uses the third person (**c**), while Paragraph B uses second person (**b**). Now, which paragraph do you find more convincing? Most people would be more convinced by paragraph B. Why?

6. Paragraph B seems more convincing because
   a. "you" puts the readers into the action of the paragraph
   b. "you" makes readers pay more attention
   c. "you" makes readers imagine themselves in that situation
   d. all of the above

The second person point of view does all of these things (**d**), and that's why it is often more convincing than the other points of view. The second person point of view puts you, as a reader, directly into the situation. As soon as you read that word *you*, you start to pay extra attention because the writer is addressing you directly. And you can't help but imagine yourself enjoying the benefits of a four-day work week because the writer puts you in each scenario. The writer of this paragraph knows that if you imagine yourself in these situations, you are much more likely to see the benefits of a four-day work week.

SUMMARY

You can see by now how important point of view is in writing, for each point of view creates a certain effect. Sometimes it brings the reader and the writer closer together; sometimes it pushes them apart. Sometimes it makes an argument more convincing through third person objectivity; sometimes an argument is more convincing through second person involvement; and sometimes it's more convincing through first person intimacy. Writers choose their point of view carefully in order to create a certain relationship both with their ideas and with the reader.

Skill Building Until Next Time

- Imagine you have an argument with someone. Tell the story of the argument, first from your point of view using the first person pronoun. Then, tell the story from the other person's point of view, again using the first person pronoun. Finally, tell the story from an outsider's point of view using the third person pronoun. Notice how the story changes when the point of view changes, and notice how both first person accounts will be subjective while the third person account is objective.

- Take a notice or letter given to you by a professor. Perhaps you have detailed instructions for a big assignment or a list of course requirements given to you at the beginning of the year. If the information addresses you in the second person *you*, change it to a third person point of view (*employees, managers, clients*). Or, if the writer uses the first person point of view (*I* or *we*), change that to the third person point of view to eliminate the subjectivity.

L·E·S·S·O·N

DICTION: WHAT'S IN A WORD?

LESSON SUMMARY

Today's lesson focuses on *diction*, the words writers choose to convey their meaning. The smallest change in choice of words can significantly change the tone and meaning of a passage. Today's lesson shows you how to pick up on the clues to meaning writers give through their choice of words.

What made Sherlock Holmes such a good detective? Was he just much smarter than everyone else? Did he have some sort of magical powers? Could he somehow see into the future or into the past? No, Sherlock Holmes was no medium or magician. So what was his secret?

His powers of observation.

You may recall that the introduction to this book talked about *active reading*. As an active reader, you should have been marking up the passages you've read in this book: identifying unfamiliar vocabulary, underlining key words and ideas, and recording your reactions and questions in the margin. But there's another part of active reading we haven't talked about: **making observations**.

MAKING OBSERVATIONS

Making observations means looking carefully at the text and noticing specific things about *how it is written.* You might notice, for example, the point of view the author has chosen. You could also notice:

- Particular words and phrases the writer uses
- The way those words and phrases are arranged in sentences and paragraphs
- Word or sentence patterns that are repeated
- Important details about people, places, and things

When you make observations, you can then make valid *inferences.* As a matter of fact, you did this in Lesson 11 when you made assumptions about how the writer wanted to be perceived based on the point of view he or she used.

OBSERVATIONS AND INFERENCES

Inferences, as you may recall, are conclusions based on reason, fact, or evidence. Good inferences come from good observations. The observations are the evidence for the inferences. Good inferences—ones based on careful observation—can help you determine meaning, as they helped Sherlock Holmes solve crimes.

To be better readers, then, we need to be more like Sherlock Holmes: We need to be better observers. In the story "The Adventure of the Blanched Soldier," Sherlock Holmes tells a client: "*I see no more than you, but I have trained myself to notice what I see.*" You don't have to be an Einstein to be a good reader; you just have to train yourself to notice what you see.

OBSERVING DICTION

Test your observation skills on the two sentences below:

A. Professor Leonard's new attendance policy, which goes into effect on Monday, should significantly reduce absenteeism.
B. Professor Leonard's draconian new attendance policy, which goes into effect on Monday, should significantly reduce absenteeism.

You don't need Sherlock Holmes's magnifying glass to see the difference between sentence A and sentence B: B uses the words *draconian* and *new* to describe the attendance policy, while A uses only *new.* (Go back to Lesson 3 if you've forgotten what *draconian* means.) Now that you have noticed this, why is it important?

1. What does sentence B tell you that sentence A doesn't?
    a. what type of policy is being discussed
    b. how the writer feels about the policy
    c. when the policy begins

The answer is **b.** Both sentences tell you that the policy is a new attendance policy, and both say that the policy goes into effect on Monday. But sentence B, because it adds the word *draconian,* tells you how the writer *feels* about the new policy: He doesn't like it. His opinion is implied through his choice of the word *draconian.* Rather than directly saying, "I think this policy is very severe," the writer *suggests* or *implies* that this is the way he feels.

DENOTATION AND CONNOTATION

Now, suppose sentence A also had another adjective to describe the new policy.

A. Professor Leonard's firm new attendance policy, which goes into effect on Monday, should significantly reduce absenteeism.

B. Professor Leonard's draconian new attendance policy, which goes into effect on Monday, should significantly reduce absenteeism.

Do the two sentences now mean the same thing? Yes and no. Both *firm* and *draconian* suggest that the policy is strict, but each word has a specific implication or suggested meaning about *how* strict that policy is. A *firm* policy is not as strict as a *draconian* policy. Furthermore, *draconian* suggests that the policy is not only strict but unfairly or unreasonably so.

So the words writers choose, even though they may mean the same thing when you look them up in the dictionary, actually have another level of meaning. This is called their **connotation**. *Connotation* is the implied meaning, the meaning that evolves when the dictionary definition (**denotation**) develops an emotional or social register or a suggestion of degree. The specific words writers choose—their *diction* or word choice—can therefore reveal a great deal about how authors feel about their subjects.

Diction: the particular words chosen and used by the author.
Denotation: exact or dictionary meaning.
Connotation: implied or suggested meaning.

HOW DICTION INFLUENCES MEANING

Put your powers of observation to work on the following sentences. Read them carefully and then write down what you notice about each writer's specific choice of words. See if you can use the writers' diction to determine what they are inferring about the seriousness of the situation they are describing.

A. The political parties are meeting with the hopes of clearing up their differences.

B. The political parties have entered into negotiations in an attempt to resolve their conflict.

Both sentences convey the same information: Two parties are meeting because they have a disagreement of some sort to address. But the differences in the diction of each sentence tell us that these two situations aren't exactly the same—or at least that the two writers have different perceptions about the situations. What differences did you notice between these two sentences? List them below (an example has been provided to get you started):

Your Observations:

Example: *I noticed that sentence A says the political parties are "meeting" whereas sentence B says they "have entered into negotiations."*

Now that you've listed your observations, answer this question: In which sentence do you think the situation is more serious, and *why* do you think so? (The *why* is especially important.)

The difference in word choice should tell you that sentence B describes the more serious situation. Here are some of the observations you might have made about the writers' diction that would have told you so.

- The political parties in sentence B are not just "meeting," they've "entered into negotiations." This phrase is often used to describe disagreements between warring parties. And "negotiations" are much more formal than "meetings," suggesting that there is a serious difference to be resolved in sentence B.
- Whereas in sentence A they are ironing things out, the parties in sentence B only "attempt to" resolve the problems. This important difference suggests that the problem between the parties in sentence A is not that serious—the problem is likely to be resolved. In sentence B, on the other hand, "in an attempt" suggests that the problem is quite serious and that it will be difficult to resolve; the outlook is doubtful rather than hopeful.
- In sentence A, the parties are seeking to "clear up their differences," whereas in sentence B, the parties want to "resolve their conflict." The phrase "clear up" suggests that there is merely some sort of confusion between the two. However, "resolve"

suggests that there is a matter that must be solved or settled. And, of course, "conflict" indicates a more serious problem than "differences."

READING BETWEEN THE LINES

Looking at diction can be especially helpful when the writer's main idea isn't quite clear. For example, in the following paragraph—an excerpt from a letter of recommendation—the author doesn't provide a topic sentence that expresses her main idea. Instead, you must use your powers of observation to answer the question about how the author feels about the student she describes.

Paragraph A

Jane Doe usually completes her work on time and checks it carefully. She is a competent speaker of the French language and is familiar with works by great French writers. She has some knowledge of the different verb tenses, and she has been a help to students who aren't quite as advanced.

2. What message does the writer of Paragraph A convey about Jane Doe?
   a. Jane Doe is an exceptional student. Admit her immediately!
   b. Jane Doe is an average student. She doesn't do outstanding work, but she won't give you any trouble.
   c. Jane Doe is a lousy student. Don't even think about admitting her.

To answer this question, you made an inference. Now, support your inference with specific observations about the language in this paragraph. Why do you think your answer is correct? (An example has been provided to get you started.)

Your Observations and Inferences:

Example: *I noticed that the writer says Jane Doe "usually" completes her work on time (observation), which suggests that Jane Doe is good but not perfect; she doesn't always get her work done on schedule (inference).*

The diction of the paragraph best supports answer **b**: The writer feels that "Jane Doe is an average student. She doesn't do outstanding work, but she won't give you any trouble." You might have supported this inference with observations like these:

- The writer uses the word *usually* in the first sentence, which means that Jane Doe is good, but not great; she doesn't always hand papers in on time.
- The writer describes Jane Doe as a "competent" speaker of the French language. This tells us that Jane Doe speaks well enough for the program, but she is not exceptional. She could be better.
- The writer tells us that Jane Doe is "familiar with" works by several great French writers. This means that she knows the names and perhaps general themes of these works, but she is no expert and may have some trouble participating in in-depth discussions.
- The writer tells us that Jane Doe has "some knowledge of the different verb tenses," which tells us that Jane Doe knows a little, but not a lot; again, she's better than someone who knows nothing, but she's no expert.

Now, take a look at a revised letter of recommendation. The diction (the word choice) has been changed so that the paragraph sends a different message. Read the paragraph carefully and determine how this writer feels about Jane Doe.

Paragraph B

Jane Doe always submits her work promptly and checks it over judiciously. She is an excellent speaker of the French language and has an in-depth knowledge of works by great French writers. She has mastered all of the different verb tenses and has been an invaluable help to students who aren't quite as advanced.

3. What message does the writer of Paragraph B convey about Jane Doe?
   a. Jane Doe is an exceptional student. Admit her immediately!
   b. Jane Doe is an average student. She doesn't do outstanding work, but she won't give you any trouble.
   c. Jane Doe is a lousy student. Don't even think about admitting her.

This time you should have chosen answer **a**. The change in diction tells you that this writer thinks Jane Doe is a fantastic student. To be sure the difference in word choice is clear, write the words the writer of Paragraph B used to replace the words in Paragraph A. The first replacement has been filled in to get you started.

Paragraph A	Paragraph B
usually	always
on time	
carefully	
competent	
is familiar with	
some knowledge	
a help	

SUMMARY

Just as Sherlock Holmes learned to notice what he saw when he arrived at the scene of a crime, you, too, can learn to notice what you see when you look carefully at a piece of writing. By noticing the specific words a writer has chosen to use, you can help ensure that you fully comprehend the writer's message.

Skill Building Until Next Time

- Think about how you choose the words you use when you speak to people. Do you use different types of words for different people? Do you think carefully about what you say and which words you will use? How much are you aware of your own diction?
- Notice how much the meaning of a sentence can change when a single word is altered. Form a simple sentence, like: "Experts say the economy is *unhealthy*." Now, replace "unhealthy" with synonyms that have slightly different connotations, like: *sick, feeble, ill, dying, under the weather, feverish, infected*. Each word will express a slightly different attitude about your subject to the reader. Insert each of these words into your sentence and see how much the meaning is altered. (This exercise will work well if you choose words like *rich, tired, happy,* or *sad* that have many synonyms with a wide range of connotations.)

13

STYLE: IT'S NOT WHAT THEY SAY BUT HOW THEY SAY IT

LESSON SUMMARY

How a writer puts words together to express meaning is as important as *what* the writer says. This lesson shows you how to analyze the style of a piece of writing in order to get a better understanding of what the writer means.

S tyle?" you ask. "What does style have to do with reading comprehension?"

Actually, style has a good deal to do with reading comprehension. Just as writers use different structures to organize their ideas and information, they also use different styles to express their ideas and information. Thus, the more aware you are of the elements of style, the more successfully you can determine a writer's purpose and understand his or her ideas.

Style is also important because it is often what attracts us to, or repels us from, certain writers or types of writing. Though an awareness of style might not make us change our taste, it can at least help us appreciate different writers and different styles.

Style: a distinctive way of writing or speaking or doing something; the manner in which something is done.

WHAT IS STYLE?

Style, in writing, generally consists of three elements:

- Sentence structure
- Degree of detail and description
- Degree of formality

Diction is also an aspect of style, but because diction is so essential to meaning, it had its own lesson in this book.

SENTENCE STRUCTURE

Looking at sentence structure means looking at the type of sentences the writer has used. Are they short, simple sentences? Or are they long and complex, with a lot of clauses and phrases? Or does the writer use a mix? Does every sentence sound the same, or is there variety in the word order and structure? Is the complexity or simplicity of the sentences at the right level for the readers?

Read the following sentences and then answer the questions that describe their sentence structure.

A. The meeting began. Mr. Thomas described the policy. Then Mr. Underwood spoke in favor of it. Afterward, Ms. Villegas spoke against it.

B. After the meeting, when everyone had already left the room, Ms. Villegas stayed behind to speak with Mr. Thomas. She carefully explained her position on the new policy, hoping she'd get him to change his mind.

1. Which version uses simple sentences?
   a. Version A
   b. Version B

2. Which version uses the same sentence structure throughout?
   a. Version A
   b. Version B

3. Which version uses complex sentences?
   a. Version A
   b. Version B

4. Which version varies the sentence structures, using different kinds of sentences?
   a. Version A
   b. Version B

You probably noticed that Version A is the one that uses simple sentences with essentially the same sentence structure throughout. (You might also have noticed that these sentences sound rather dull because they are so simple and unvaried.) In Version B, the sentences are far more complex with more variation in their structure.

DEGREE OF DETAIL AND DESCRIPTION

When you look at degree of detail and description, ask two things:

1. How specific is the author? Does he write "dog" (general) or "Labrador retriever" (specific detail)? Does she write "some" (general) or "three and a half pounds" (specific detail)?

2. How much description does the author provide? Does he write "Mr. B is my manager" (nondescriptive) or "Mr. B, my manager, is a

tall man with piercing eyes and a mustache" (descriptive)? Or does he go even further: "Mr. B, my manager, is six foot ten with eyes that pierce like knives and a mustache like Hitler's" (very descriptive)?

Try your hand at deciding whether words are specific and descriptive or general and nondescriptive.

5. Which words or phrases below are more specific and descriptive? Underline them. Which words or phrases are more general and nondescriptive? Circle them.

    a. car

    b. red 1968 Ford

    c. on the corner of 58th and Broadway

    d. on the corner

As you could probably tell, answers **b** and **c** are the more specific and descriptive ones, while answers **a** and **d** are more general and nondescriptive.

DEGREE OF FORMALITY

The **degree of formality** of a piece of writing has to do with how formal or casual the writer's language is. For example, does the writer use slang as if speaking to a friend, or jargon (specific, technical language) as if speaking to colleagues? Does the writer address the reader by his or her first name (casual), or by his or her title (formal)?

Decide whether the following sentences are formal or informal.

6. Which sentences below are more informal? Underline them. Which are more formal? Circle them.

    a. Let's get together after work on Thursday.

    b. We kindly request that you join us for a social gathering at the close of business on Thursday.

    c. These figures indicate the sales have increased significantly.

    d. Sales are up!

Chances are that you didn't have much trouble deciding that sentences **a** and **d** are more informal and sentences **b** and **c** are more formal.

HOW THE THREE ELEMENTS OF STYLE WORK TOGETHER

Look at how these three elements of style work together in the following examples. Below are two different letters. Both convey essentially the same information, but they are written in radically different styles. Read the letters carefully and then list your observations. What do you notice that's different between these two letters?

Letter A

Bob:

Listen, a while ago we rush ordered some paper from you. We haven't gotten it yet. What happened? Where is it? Find out! We need it!

—Joe

Letter B

Dear Mr. Brown:

Three weeks ago, on January 22, we rush ordered two dozen boxes of XYZ bond paper from you (Order #123456). To date we have not received our order. Please look into this matter immediately as we are in dire need of this product.

Sincerely,

Mr. White

What did you notice about these two letters? How are they different? Consider sentence structure, degree of description and detail, and degree of formality. List your observations below (an example has been provided to get you started):

Your Observations:

Example: *I notice that Letter A addresses the reader as "Bob" whereas Letter B addresses him as "Mr. Brown."*

Now, answer the following questions.

7. Which letter is more formal?
   a. Letter A
   b. Letter B

8. Which letter seems to have been written by someone who knows the recipient well?
   a. Letter A
   b. Letter B

9. In which letter is the sentence structure more complex?
   a. Letter A
   b. Letter B

10. Which letter is more descriptive and detailed?
   a. Letter A
   b. Letter B

You probably noticed immediately the difference in degree of formality between these two letters. Letter A is written in a very casual style, as if the writer knows the reader very well and therefore does not need to use a professional approach. Our first clue to this casual relationship is the way the letter is addressed. Letter A addresses the reader as "Bob" while letter B begins with a formal "Dear Mr. Brown." The same difference can be seen in the closing of the letters: "Joe" vs. "Sincerely, Mr. White."

The (in)formality of each relationship is also reflected in the sentence structure and degree of description and detail. You probably noticed, for example, that Letter A uses short, choppy sentences, and exclamation points, which make the letter sound less formal, more urgent, and more demanding. The writer also uses casual words like "listen" so that the writing sounds conversational. On the other hand, Letter B uses longer, more complex sentences to make the letter sound more formal and sophisticated.

At the same time you probably noticed that letter A does not provide specific information as Letter B does. Letter A tells us the writer placed an order for "some paper" "a while ago," but Letter B tells us the order was placed "three weeks ago, on January 22" and that the order was for "two dozen boxes of XYZ bond paper." The fact that Letter A does not provide specific details is further evidence that the reader knows the writer very well, for the writer doesn't have to provide specific details. Furthermore, in Letter A the writer uses a command—"Find out!"—whereas in Letter B, the writer *asks*, rather than demands, that the matter be looked into. This politeness reflects a professional distance between writer and reader.

In business, as in most writing, the audience usually determines the writer's style. The writer of Letter A is probably capable of writing in the style of Letter B, but because he has a casual relationship with his reader, he doesn't need to use a formal style.

THE EFFECT OF DESCRIPTION AND DETAIL

In business, what some people call "flowery" style—lots of description and detail—is almost never appropriate. Why? Because in business, as they say, "time is money," so readers don't want to spend time reading lengthy descriptions or extensive detail. They just want the facts: when the meeting will be held and where; what the new product is designed to do and how much it costs; how the new training manual is coming along. In most cases, the more straightforward, the better.

Other times, however, when they want readers to imagine a situation or to experience something through language, writers need a "flowery" style. That is, they need a high degree of description and detail. The two paragraphs below show the difference. Both describe the same business meeting, but in two very different styles. One is written in a style appropriate to business and only records the facts. The other describes the meeting in a style appropriate for general readers interested in the feelings of the employee, Mr. Newman.

Paragraph A

Yesterday at 9:00 A.M., Mr. Owen called Mr. Newman into his office. Mr. Owen reviewed Mr. Newman's personnel file. He congratulated Mr. Newman on his perfect attendance record and consistently satisfactory reviews. Then Mr. Owen informed Mr. Newman that his position, along with several others, was being eliminated due to a restructuring of the company. Mr. Owen offered Mr. Newman three months severance pay and continuation of benefits for one year.

Paragraph B

At 9:00 A.M., Mr. Owen raised a thick arm to wave Mr. Newman into his office. Mr. Newman obeyed reluctantly and sat stiffly in front of the monstrous oak desk that managed to dwarf even Mr. Owen, a bulky man with a protruding stomach. Mr. Newman fidgeted as Mr. Owen opened his personnel file. Then, after praising Mr. Newman for his years of perfect attendance and his continuously satisfactory reviews, Mr. Owen told Mr. Newman that his position—which he had had for over fourteen years—was being eliminated. The company was being restructured and Mr. Newman's job was no longer necessary.

Mr. Owen went on to explain that Mr. Newman would have three months of severance pay and a year of continued benefits, but Mr. Newman didn't hear him. He walked out of Mr. Owen's office before Mr. Owen could finish his sentence.

Now, write down your observations about these two paragraphs below. How are these two versions different? What did you notice about the sentence structure? About the degree of description and detail? About the degree of formality?

Your Observations:

Example: *I noticed that Version B is almost twice as long as Version A.*

Now, use your observations to answer the following questions.

11. Which version tells you more about Mr. Owen?
a. Paragraph A
b. Paragraph B

12. Which version tells you more about Mr. Newman?
a. Paragraph A
b. Paragraph B

13. Which version is more objective?
a. Paragraph A
b. Paragraph B

14. Which version makes you feel badly for Mr. Newman?
a. Paragraph A
b. Paragraph B

You noticed, of course, that Paragraph B is much more descriptive than Paragraph A—it tells you more about both Mr. Owen and Mr. Newman. Paragraph A just provides the facts—specific details, but no description. Paragraph A is very objective. We do not know what Mr. Owen looks like or how Mr. Newman feels (though we might be able to guess).

Paragraph B, however, tells us about Mr. Owen's appearance (he's a "thick," "bulky" man with a "protruding stomach"); we know about his desk (it's "monstrous"). More importantly, we know how Mr. Newman felt about the meeting and the news he received. Obviously, Mr. Newman knew he was going to get bad news; he entered the office "reluctantly" and "fidgeted" in his chair. Of course, he was very upset by the news, which he demonstrated by walking out of the room before Mr. Owen could finish. These details help us feel something for Mr. Newman because the characters and the situation are presented visually; we can almost see what happens.

SUMMARY

Style, as you can see, is an important aspect of reading comprehension. It can tell us about the writer's relationship to the reader; it can distance us with its objectivity or draw us in with its description and detail. As readers, we tend to react strongly to style, often without knowing why. But now you do know why, and you can use that knowledge to help you understand what you read.

Skill Building Until Next Time

- As you come across sentences or paragraphs written in different styles, see how they would sound if the style were altered. Change the level of formality, the degree of description and detail, or the sentence structure to create a new style.
- Do you have a favorite author? Take a second look at a particularly memorable work by this author, paying close attention to the style elements at work. If you are a Jane Austen fan, pick out features that make her novels enjoyable for you. Do you like her degree of formality, the way she uses detail to describe fancy parties, or the way she varies her sentence structure? After you've taken a close look at this work, try your own hand at it. Can you write a letter to a friend in the same style that Jane Austen would have? How about Ernest Hemingway or Stephen King?

L·E·S·S·O·N 14

HOW THEY SAY IT, PART TWO: TONE

LESSON SUMMARY

The way you perceive a person's tone of voice has a great deal to do with how you understand what that person is saying. The same is true of tone in writing; it's vital to pick up on clues to tone in order to understand a written piece fully. This lesson shows you how.

Say this word out loud: "Sure."

How did you say it? Did you say it with a smile, as in "Sure, any time"? Or did you say it flatly, as if responding to a command? Or did you stretch the word out, "*Suuuurre*," as if you didn't believe what someone just said? Or did you ask it, as in, "Are you *sure* this is okay?"

Perhaps you didn't realize there were so many ways to say this one single word, "sure." But there are. Why? The word itself isn't different; its denotation (dictionary meaning) isn't different; so how can the same word express so many different things?

The difference in the meaning of all of these *sure*s comes from the tone—how you say the word, and thus how your listeners will feel when they hear you say it.

Tone: the mood or attitude conveyed by words or speech.

When you speak and listen, you can hear the tone of your own and the other's voice. But how do you catch tone in writing? How do you know how the writer wants his or her words to sound? "Sure" by itself doesn't tell us whether you should whisper or shout it out. You need to look at the context surrounding that word to find clues about the proper tone to use.

Think about how tone is created in speech. When you say "sure," the tone changes according to how loudly or softly you say the word and how slowly or quickly you say it. Tone is also conveyed (or supported) by the speaker's expressions and body language. In writing, of course, you do not have these visual resources, but you do have plenty of clues to help you determine tone. Those clues come from the elements of language and style that you've studied so far: point of view, diction, and style.

HOW TONE INFLUENCES MEANING

It may help you to think of a sentence as a collection of ingredients (words and phrases) that result in a dish (idea). These elements of language and style are like the spices that you need to give that sentence a certain flavor. Different spices will result in a different flavor (tone).

Look at the two letters below. Both convey essentially the same information, but they have two rather different tones.

Letter A
Dear Client:

Thank you for your letter. We will take your suggestion into consideration. We appreciate your concern.

Letter B
Dear Valued Customer:

Thank you for your recent letter regarding our refund policy and procedure. We are taking your suggestion quite seriously and truly appreciate your concern.

Which of these letters has a more positive tone? As you can see, Letter B is more positive. Why? What do you notice about Letter B that is different from Letter A? List your observations below:

Your Observations:
Example: *I noticed that Letter A is addressed "Dear Client" while Letter B is addressed "Dear Valued Customer."*

Perhaps you noticed that Letter B uses key words like "*valued* customer" and "*truly* appreciate." Letter B also refers to the specific contents of the reader's letter, thus letting the reader know that his or her letter has been read. Furthermore, Letter B tells the reader not just that the company "will take your suggestion into consideration"—which sounds a bit like an empty promise—but that the writers are taking the suggestion "quite seriously."

You may also notice that the sentences in Letter B are longer than those in Letter A, whose sentences are shorter and somewhat choppy. If you read those short sentences out loud, how do they sound? They're not very inviting, are they? They sound somewhat mechanical and empty of any feeling.

Use your observations to answer the questions below.

1. The tone of Letter A is best classified as
   a. sincere
   b. complimentary
   c. indifferent

Choice c, indifferent, best describes the tone of Letter A. There is no indication that the writers of Letter A have actually read their client's letter, so there's no indication that they plan to take the client's suggestion seriously. They are indifferent to it. Also, the sentence structure indicates that the writers have not put much thought into writing this letter; as a result, the sentences sound abrupt and even unappreciative.

2. The tone of letter B is best classified as
   a. cheerful
   b. sincere
   c. apologetic

In contrast to Letter A, the writers of Letter B are b, sincere. They know exactly what their customer wrote about—there's the importance of specific details again! They've also taken the time to individualize the letter; and they've added words that show they value their customer and their customer's feedback.

VARIETIES OF TONE

Just as there are endless varieties of tone when we speak, there are endless varieties of tone in writing.

Here's a short list of some of the more common words used to describe a writer's tone:

cheerful	sarcastic
complimentary	ironic
hopeful	wistful
sad	foreboding
gloomy	playful
apologetic	sincere
critical	insincere
insecure	authoritative
disrespectful	threatening
humorous	indifferent

If any of these terms are unfamiliar to you, please look them up in a dictionary right away.

PRACTICE

Now look at several sentences and paragraphs to see if you can correctly identify their tone. As you read them, think of how the paragraphs sound. You may even want to read them out loud. With what kind of voice do you read? What's your tone? Use your instincts, as well as your observations, to choose the correct tone for each paragraph. Answers and explanations come immediately after the practice paragraphs.

3. I think the theme of this novel probably has something to do with revenge.
   a. playful
   b. uncertain
   c. cheerful

4. Without a doubt, the theme of this novel is revenge.
   a. gloomy
   b. disrespectful
   c. authoritative

5. Your essay? Oh, it was just fabulous. Really, I've never seen anything like it.
   a. insincere
   b. critical
   c. disrespectful

6. This is one of the best essays I've ever seen. It's clear, concise, and convincing.
   a. complimentary
   b. wistful
   c. hopeful

7. Bill had stayed up all night preparing for this presentation. He had everything ready: charts, graphs, lists, statistics. This was the biggest meeting of his career. He was ready. He smiled as the cab pulled up to 505 Park Avenue, and he gave the taxi driver an extra large tip. He entered the building confidently and pushed #11 on the elevator. Suddenly, as the doors of the elevator closed, he realized that he had left his briefcase in the cab.
   a. cheerful
   b. ironic
   c. critical

Answers and Explanations

3. b. The writer is obviously afraid to be authoritative and uses phrases like "I think," "probably," and "something to do with," to reflect this uncertainty.

4. c. The writer is clearly comfortable in making a definitive statement. There is no hesitation in the tone here. Instead of suggesting, the writer declares: "Without a doubt…."

5. a. Because of the opening question and because the next sentences are so vague, a reader can assume that the writer either hasn't read the essay or didn't like it. Also, "really" indicates that the writer is afraid the reader won't be convinced by the statement, so he tries to emphasize it. Furthermore, "I've never seen anything like it" isn't necessarily a compliment—it could really mean many different things, not all of them good.

6. a. Unlike question 5 above, this paragraph really is complimentary. The writer specifies three things that make the reader's essay exceptional: It's "clear, concise and convincing." The use of more specific adjectives makes this writer's praise seem sincere.

7. b. *Irony* is the mood created when things happen in a manner that is opposite of what was expected to happen. Here, Bill had prepared diligently for the big meeting and had everything ready. But contrary to his expectations of having a very successful presentation, he had no presentation at all because he left his materials in the taxi cab. The irony is heightened by his confidence.

SUMMARY

An ability to determine tone is an essential component of reading comprehension. Often, writers will let their tone convey their meaning, so you need to look carefully for clues in the writer's language and style to determine how writers want their words to sound.

Skill Building Until Next Time

- Listen carefully to people today and notice how much you depend on tone to determine exactly what people mean when they speak to you. Notice also how you use tone to convey meaning when you speak to other people.
- Go back to the practice exercise where you identified the tone of those five passages. Try changing the tone of some of those passages.

L·E·S·S·O·N

WORD POWER: PUTTING IT ALL TOGETHER

15

LESSON SUMMARY

This lesson pulls together what you've learned in Lessons 11–14, as well as in previous lessons. It shows you how to use point of view, diction, style, and tone to understand what a writer means.

You've learned a lot this week about language and how much it affects meaning. Before you add this knowledge to the knowledge you already have about structure and the basics of reading comprehension, take a minute for a brief review of the last four lessons.

REVIEW: LANGUAGE AND STYLE

Point of view is the perspective from which the writer speaks. Sometimes writers use the first person point of view (*I, me, my, we, our, us*) to express their personal feelings and experiences directly to the reader. This point of view creates a sense of intimacy between the reader and the writer because it expresses an extremely subjective perspective. When writers use the second person point of view, they address the reader directly by using the pronoun *you*. This point of view is often used to give directions and to make the reader feel directly involved in the action described by the writer. The third person point of view is the objective perspective of a "third person," someone who is not directly involved in the action or ideas expressed in the passage. This point of view establishes a distance between the reader and writer and uses the pronouns *he, his, him, she, hers, her, it, its, they, them,* and *their*.

Diction refers to the specific words chosen by the author to express his or her ideas. Because words have both a *denotation* (exact or dictionary meaning) and a *connotation* (implied or suggested meaning), as well as an emotional register, the words an author chooses are very significant. Authors, like politicians, must choose their words carefully to express exactly the right idea with exactly the right impact.

Style is the manner in which the writers express their ideas in writing. Style is composed of three main elements: sentence structure, degree of description and detail, and degree of formality. Some writers use a very formal style; others may write in a casual style. Certain styles are best for particular audiences or purposes. For example, a high degree of formality with specific details but without any unneccessary description would be appropriate for business, where time is money and writers should get to the point as quickly as possible.

Finally, **tone** is the mood or attitude conveyed by the writing. Tone is created by a combination of point of view, diction, and style. Tone is extremely important in determining meaning because as we noted, a word as simple as "sure" can have many different meanings depending upon the tone in which it is said. To determine the tone, you have to look for clues as to how the writer wants his or her words to sound.

If any of these terms or ideas sound unfamiliar to you, STOP. Please take a few minutes to review whatever lesson is unclear.

PRACTICE

In today's practice, you'll combine the above aspects of language with everything else you've learned in this book about reading comprehension:

- Finding the facts
- Determining the main idea
- Determining vocabulary meaning through context
- Distinguishing facts and opinions
- Chronological order
- Cause and effect
- Compare and contrast
- Order of importance

PRACTICE PASSAGE 1

Begin with a paragraph someone might see in a company newsletter: a profile of a company executive. Read the paragraph carefully, marking it up as you go, and write your observations in the space provided.

Ms. A has been a dedicated employee since the company opened its doors in 1978. She started out as a clerk and quickly moved up in the ranks to become a branch manager in 1987. Her innovative revision of the marketing plan in 1988 doubled company profits within a year and earned her the position of Junior Vice President. Today she is a Senior Vice President who continues to contribute cutting-edge ideas and dedication to the company.

Your Observations:

Now answer the following questions.

1. Ms. A became a branch manager in
   a. 1987
   b. 1988
   c. 1978

2. Which sentence best sums up the main idea of this paragraph?
   a. Ms. A is a very smart.
   b. Ms. A is very dedicated.
   c. The company would be nowhere without Ms. A.

3. "Ms. A has been a dedicated employee since the company opened its doors in 1978" is
   a. fact
   b. opinion
   c. point of view

4. "Innovative" means
   a. helpful
   b. remarkable
   c. inventive

5. This paragraph is organized according to what structure?
   a. cause and effect
   b. compare and contrast
   c. chronological order
   d. order of importance

6. This paragraph uses what point of view?
   a. First person point of view
   b. Second person point of view
   c. Third person point of view

Answers

1. **a.** "She started out as a clerk and quickly moved up in the ranks to become a branch manager in 1987."

2. **b.** While it does seem that Ms. A must be very smart since she has had such success with the company, that is not the idea that governs the whole paragraph. Instead, the paragraph highlights her dedication by showing that she has been with the company since its beginning. Answer **c** can't be correct because, although the paragraph indicates that Ms. A is very valuable, it does not say that the company would be nowhere without her. This is an inference you might make but cannot support.

3. **b.** Although the sentence does contain fact (she started with the company in 1978), the sentence makes an assertion about those years since 1978: that Ms. A has been dedicated all those years. This is an assertion, an opinion that needs evidence. The rest of the paragraph goes on to provide that evidence.

4. **c.** The best clue to determining the meaning of this word is found in the last sentence, which says that Ms. A "continues to contribute cutting-edge ideas" to the company. Since the paragraph only mentions one specific contribution (the one labeled "innovative"), we can assume that *innovative* means *cutting-edge* or *inventive*.

5. **c.** The paragraph follows Ms. A's career with the company from its start in 1978 to the present.

6. **c.** This paragraph uses the objective third person point of view. There is no *I* or *we* (first person) or *you* (second person), and the only pronouns the paragraph uses are the third person pronouns *she* and *her*.

How did you do? If you got all six answers correct, good work. The table below shows you which lesson to study for each question you missed.

If you missed:	Then study:
Question 1	Lesson 1
Question 2	Lesson 2
Question 3	Lesson 4
Question 4	Lesson 3
Question 5	Lesson 6
Question 6	Lesson 11

PRACTICE PASSAGE 2

Now try another paragraph. Don't forget to mark it up as you read and make observations. Pay special attention to language and style.

There will be dire consequences for students if the state goes through with the proposed budget cuts. First of all, the cuts will mean that many of us will have to change majors since the arts departments do not hold academic precedence in the eyes of the board of trustees. Second, many of us will be forced to drop out and get jobs since financial aid will be reduced considerably. But most importantly, the budget cuts mean that the quality of education for those of us who remain will suffer drastically.

7. The main idea of this passage is that the budget cuts would
   a. be great for the university
   b. not change things much
   c. be bad for students

8. "Precedence" means
   a. priority of importance
   b. degree of difficulty
   c. amount of financial profit

9. This passage is organized
   a. in chronological order
   b. by cause and effect
   c. by order of importance
   d. both a and c
   e. both b and c

10. This passage uses which point of view?
   a. first person
   b. second person
   c. third person

11. This passage is written from whose perspective?
   a. that of the professors
   b. that of the students
   c. that of an outside consultant

12. The choice of the word *dire* suggests that the consequences of the budget cuts would be
   a. minimal
   b. expected
   c. disastrous

13. Which word best describes the style of this passage?
   a. informal, conversational
   b. descriptive, story-like
   c. formal, business-like

14. The tone of this passage is
   a. sad
   b. foreboding
   c. threatening

Answers

7. **c.** The first sentence is the topic sentence, which establishes that the budget cuts will be bad for students. The remaining sentences support that idea.

8. **a.** The word "academic" should tell you that choice c is not correct, and knowing that the board of trustees would be more concerned with level of importance than with degree of difficulty should tell you that choice b is not correct.

9. **e.** The writer warns readers of the effects budget cuts would have on students and arranges those effects in order of importance, saving the most important effect for last.

10. **a.** The first person point of view is reflected in the use of the pronoun *us* and *we*.

11. **b.** The writer says that the budget cuts will have "dire consequences" for the students and then uses the pronouns *us* and *we*—identifying himself with the students—when listing those dire consequences.

12. **c.** The effects the writer includes here are all very serious, especially the third effect—the decrease in quality of education. The writer has chosen the word *dire* to emphasize that seriousness.

13. **c.** The passage avoids any unnecessary description or details and uses formal rather than casual language.

14. **b.** Each sentence explains a negative effect that the budget cuts will have on the students, and the negativity of this passage is heightened by the words "dire" and "suffer drastically." Though the budget cut itself might be described as *threatening* (choice c), the writer is not threatening anybody.

How did you do? Once again, congratulations if you got them all correct. If not, the table below tells you what to do.

If you missed:	Then study:
Question 7	Lesson 2
Question 8	Lesson 3
Question 9	Lessons 7 and 9
Question 10	Lesson 11
Question 11	Lesson 11
Question 12	Lesson 12
Question 13	Lesson 13
Question 14	Lesson 14

Skill Building Until Next Time

- Review the Skill Building sections from Lessons 6–14. Try any Skill Builders you didn't do.
- Write a paragraph about what you've learned in the last two weeks about structure and language. Begin your paragraph with a clear topic sentence, such as "I've learned a lot about how writers use structure and language." Then, write several sentences that support or explain your assertion. Try to use at least one new vocabulary word in your paragraph.

READING BETWEEN THE LINES

Now that you've studied the way authors use structure and language to organize and express their ideas, you're ready to tackle more difficult passages: those in which the writers don't provide clear topic sentences or do not clearly indicate their intentions. To understand this type of text, you have to "read between the lines." This means you have to really put your observation skills to use and scour the passage for clues to meaning. Like Sherlock Holmes, you will really have to notice what you see.

By the end of this section, you should be able to:

- Determine an implied main idea
- Determine an implied cause or effect
- Distinguish between logical and emotional appeals
- Use your reading skills to help you think critically
- Determine the theme of a piece of literature
- Understand the differences in reading for various college courses

You'll look at a variety of texts, including some literature, and then put it all together in a review lesson. Finally, Lesson 23 gives you tips on using your newly strengthened reading skills to help you prepare for and take exams.

FINDING THE IMPLIED MAIN IDEA

16

LESSON SUMMARY

This lesson shows you how to determine the main idea of a passage in which the writer has not provided a topic sentence or otherwise spelled it out for you.

O h, the power of suggestion. Advertisers know it well—and so do writers. They know that they can get an idea across to their readers without directly saying it. Instead of providing a topic sentence that expresses their main idea, many times they simply omit that sentence and instead provide a series of clues through structure and language to get their ideas across.

Finding an implied main idea is much like finding a stated main idea. If you recall from Lesson 2, a main idea is defined as an assertion about the subject that controls or holds together all of the ideas in the passage. Therefore, the main idea must be general enough to encompass all of the ideas in the passage. Much like a net, it holds everything in the passage together. So far, all but one of the passages in this book have had a topic sentence that stated the main idea, so finding the main idea was something of a process of elimination: You could eliminate the sentences that weren't general enough to encompass the whole passage. But what do you do when there's no topic sentence?

You use your observations to make an inference—this time, an inference about the main idea or point of the passage.

HOW TO FIND AN IMPLIED MAIN IDEA

Finding an implied main idea requires you to use your observations to make an inference that, like a topic sentence, encompasses the whole passage. It might take a little detective work, but now that you know how to find details and how to understand word choice, style, and tone, you can make observations that will enable you to find main ideas even when they're not explicitly stated.

PRACTICE PASSAGE 1

For the first example of finding an implied main idea, let's return to our friend Mr. Blank. If you remember, back in Lesson 1 his apartment was robbed. Now look at a statement from the building manager in response to news of the robbery:

> This is the third robbery in our building this month. Each time, the thieves have gotten past building security with almost the entire contents of the victim's apartment. Yet each time, the security officers say they have seen nothing unusual.

> Now, there is no topic sentence in this paragraph, but you should be able to determine the manager's main idea from the facts he provides and from his tone. What is he suggesting?

1. Which of the following best summarizes the manager's main idea?
   a. There are too many robberies in the building.
   b. There are not enough security officers in the building.
   c. There is something wrong with the security in the building.

Answer

The correct answer is **c**, "There is something wrong with the security in the building." How can you tell that this is the main idea? For one thing, it's the only one of the three choices that is general enough to serve as a "net" for the paragraph; choice **a** is implied only in the first sentence and choice **b** isn't mentioned at all. In addition, each sentence on its own suggests that security in the building has not been working properly. Furthermore, the word "yet" indicates that there is a conflict between the events that have taken place and the duties of the security officers.

PRACTICE PASSAGE 2

Now examine the following statement from Mr. Blank's neighbor, who was also interviewed after the robbery:

> Well, Mr. Blank's a pretty carefree man. A few times I've knocked on his door and he just hollers, "Come in," and I just have to push the door open because it isn't locked. He often forgets things, too, like where he parked his car or where he put his keys. One time I found him in the hall searching through his bags because he couldn't find his keys, and it turned out the door was open anyway. Sometimes I wonder how he remembers to eat, let alone to take care of his apartment.

2. What is Mr. Blank's neighbor suggesting?
   a. Mr. Blank forgets everything.
   b. Mr. Blank may have left his door open that day.
   c. Mr. Blank is too carefree for his own good.

> You can attack the question this way: Which of these three statements do the sentences in the neighbor's statement support? Try a process of elimination. Do all of the sentences support choice **a**? If not, cross **a** out. Do all of the sentences support choice **b**? Choice **c**?

Answer

The correct answer is **b,** "Mr. Blank may have left his door open that day." How can you tell? Because this is the only idea that all of the sentences in the neighbor's statement support. You know that Mr. Blank often doesn't lock his door when he's home; you also know that he often forgets things. Thus, the neighbor's statement contains both **a** and **c,** but neither can be the main idea because the neighbor discusses both things in combination. This combination makes it likely that Mr. Blank left his apartment door open on the day he was robbed.

PRACTICE PASSAGE 3

Now look at a paragraph in which the *language* the writer uses is what enables you to determine meaning. Back in Lesson 13, you read a thumbnail sketch of Mr. B the manager. Below is a more detailed version of that description. Read the following paragraph carefully and see if you can determine the implied main idea of the paragraph.

> Mr. B, my manager, is six feet ten inches tall with eyes that pierce like knives and a mustache like Hitler's. He invades the office at precisely 8:00 every morning demanding this report and that report. He spends half of the day looking over my shoulder and barking orders. And whenever there's a mistake— even if it's his fault—he blames it on me.

Before you decide on the implied main idea, list your observations. What did you notice about the language in this paragraph? An example is provided to get you started.

Your Observations:

> **Example:** *I noticed that Mr. B's eyes are compared to knives.*

3. Which of the following best expresses the implied message of the passage?
   a. Working for Mr. B is a challenge.
   b. Working for Mr. B is like working for a tyrant.
   c. Mr. B is a terrible manager.

Answer

The correct answer is **b,** "Working for Mr. B is like working for a tyrant." There are many clues in the language of this paragraph that lead you to this inference. First, you probably noticed that Mr. B "has eyes that pierce like knives." This comparison (called a *simile*) suggests that Mr. B does not look at others very warmly; instead, his eyes stab.

Second, the description of Mr. B's mustache is a critical part of the way the author establishes the tone of this paragraph. To say that Mr. B has a mustache "like Hitler's" automatically makes us picture Mr. B as Hitler. This is a very serious comparison (also a simile). A writer wouldn't compare someone to Hitler—even on a physical level—unless he wanted to paint that person as evil.

Third, the author tells us that Mr. B "invades" the office at "precisely" 8:00 every morning. "Invade" is a key word choice. The author could have said that Mr. B "storms into" the office or "barges into" the office, but he chose the word "invades," as if Mr. B doesn't belong there or as if Mr. B is attempting to take over territory that isn't his. Furthermore, Mr. B spends the day "barking orders," and, like a tyrant, he passes the blame onto others when something goes wrong. Thus, though answers **a** and **c** may be true—it must be a challenge to work with Mr. B, and he doesn't seem to be the best "people person"—answer **b** is the only idea that all of the sentences in the paragraph support.

Of course, this person's description of Mr. B is very subjective, using as it does the first person point of view. As an active reader, you should wonder whether everyone sees Mr. B this way or if this employee is unable to be objective about Mr. B.

PRACTICE PASSAGE 4

Many people find reading literature a difficult task because in literature (fiction, drama, and poetry), the main idea is almost never expressed in a clear topic sentence. Instead, readers have to look for clues that are often hidden in the language of the text. For example, the following fictional paragraph describes a character. Read it carefully, make your observations, and then identify the main idea of the paragraph.

In the evening when Dell finished a long day at work, she came home alone to an empty house. She'd make herself a small tasteless supper—she never felt like cooking anymore, now that there was no one else but her to feed. At night she'd tend to the animals in the back and would often talk to them to break the silence that imprisoned her.

Your Observations:

Example: *I noticed that Dell is the only person mentioned in this paragraph.*

4. The main idea of this paragraph is that
   a. Dell wants to be alone
   b. Dell was abandoned
   c. Dell is very lonely

Answer

Although it is possible that **b**, "Dell was abandoned," there is no evidence in this paragraph to support that inference. Thus, **b** cannot be the main idea. Answer **a**, "Dell wants to be alone," cannot be correct either, since everything in the paragraph suggests that Dell does *not* like to be alone: She doesn't like to cook anymore now that she's alone, and she talks to the animals because there's no one else for her to talk to.

Furthermore, the language of the paragraph creates a feeling of intense loneliness: Dell comes home "alone" to an "empty" house; her dinner is "tasteless"; she talks to the animals "to break the silence that imprison[s] her." All of these words work together in the paragraph to create a feeling of loneliness. Thus, without directly saying so, the writer tells us that **c**, "Dell is very lonely."

SUMMARY

Many writers use implication to convey meaning rather than directly stating their ideas. This is especially true in literature, where readers generally prefer suggestion to direct statements. Finding the implied main idea requires a little detective work, but it is not as difficult as you may have thought, now that you know more about language and the way words can be used to suggest ideas.

Skill Building Until Next Time

- Listen carefully to people today. Are there times when they *imply* things without directly saying them? Are there times when *you* use suggestion to get your ideas across? How do you do this? Be aware of how you and others use indirect language and suggestion to convey meaning.

- Write a paragraph that does not have a topic sentence. You should have a clear idea of the main idea before you write your paragraph and make sure your sentences use language that will help your readers understand your main idea. For example, think of a topic sentence about the kind of person you are, but don't write it down. Then, write several sentences that support your topic sentence with language that leads your reader to the proper conclusion. You may want to show your paragraph to others to see if they can correctly infer your main idea.

L·E·S·S·O·N

ASSUMING CAUSES AND PREDICTING EFFECTS

17

LESSON SUMMARY

Today's lesson focuses on how to determine cause and effect when they are only implied, rather than explicitly stated.

ave you ever regretted just "telling it like it is"? Many times you can't come right out and say what you'd like, but, like writers, you can get your ideas across through *implication* or inference.

This lesson focuses on two specific types of implication: reading between the lines to *determine cause* and reading between the lines to *predict effects*.

In case you need a reminder: A *cause* is the person or thing that makes something happen or produces an effect. An *effect* is the change that occurs as a result of some action or cause. Cause tells us why something happened; effect tells us what happened after a cause (or series of causes).

DETERMINING IMPLIED CAUSES

In order to see how to determine causes that are implied rather than stated, look at the following brief fictional passage. Read the passage carefully and actively. After you make your observations, see if you can use the writer's clues to determine why the characters are fighting.

Ann tensed when she heard the keys jingle in the door. She waited at the kitchen table; she knew Jim would check the kitchen first. She took a deep breath, thought again about what she would say, and waited.

A moment later Jim stepped into the kitchen. She watched as his mouth started to form the word "hello" but then changed abruptly when he saw that last night's dishes were still piled high in the sink. His handsome face hardened with anger. Pointing a calloused finger at the perilously stacked dishes, he said calmly, coldly, "What are those filthy things still doing in the sink?"

"I haven't gotten to them yet," she replied, equally cold.

"How many times have I told you I want this house clean when I come home?"

"Oh, every day. You tell me every blessed day. In fact, you tell me every day exactly what I should do and how I should do it. Do you think that just because you married me you own me?"

"I do own this house, that's for sure. And I want my house clean!" he shouted.

"Then hire a maid," she said sarcastically.

"What?"

"You heard me. Hire a maid. That is, if you can find one who can stand to work for someone who is never satisfied."

Look carefully at the dialogue between these two characters. What do they say to each other? How is it said? What other clues from the author can you find in this passage to help you understand the cause of their conflict? List your observations below and then answer the questions that follow.

Your Observations:

Example: *I noticed that Ann was in the kitchen waiting for Jim as if she had planned this confrontation.*

1. Why does Jim get angry?
   a. because Ann didn't get up to meet him at the door
   b. because he had had a bad day at work
   c. because Ann didn't do the dishes

2. Why didn't Ann do the dishes?
   a. because she didn't have time to do them
   b. because she wanted to start a fight
   c. because she was too lazy

3. Why is Ann angry at Jim?
   a. because he didn't say hello when he walked in
   b. because he is impossible to please
   c. because they don't have a maid to do the housework

Answers

1. c. You can tell that Jim is angry because Ann didn't wash the dishes because when he sees the dishes in the sink, his face "harden[s] in anger." You can also tell that he is angry about the dishes because he asks Ann, "What are those filthy things still doing in the sink?"—indicating that he had expected them to be done. The tone of his voice—"calmly, coldly"—indicates that he is very angry but trying to control his anger. Furthermore, he exclaims that he wants his house clean when he comes home, so you can safely assume that he is angry that the dishes are still dirty.

2. b. Though Ann *says* she didn't get to the dishes (answer **a**), the fact that she's sitting at the table rather than washing dishes indicates that something else is going on. Evidently Ann has planned this confrontation, since she's "wait[ing] at the kitchen table," expecting Jim to come home. The passage also says that Ann "thought *again* about what she would say, and waited." This indicates that she has been thinking about what to say to Jim when he saw that she hadn't done the dishes.

3. b. You can tell that Ann is angry because she thinks Jim is impossible to please when she says, "Oh, every day. You tell me every blessed day. In fact, you tell me every day exactly what I should do and how to do it." The tone of her response is very angry; she is fed up with being told what to do. Furthermore, she challenges him to find a maid "who can stand to work for someone who is never satisfied." These clues tell us that Jim is difficult to please.

A Look at the Effects of the Causes

Clearly, in the passage above, Ann had a certain effect in mind when she decided not to do the dishes: She wanted a confrontation. Now, based on what you've seen of this couple so far, answer the following question about the effect Ann might have been looking for.

4. In provoking a confrontation, Ann most likely hoped that Jim would
   a. do the dishes himself for once
   b. hire a maid to help her take care of the house
   c. become less demanding and more appreciative

The best answer is **c**, she wants Jim to become less demanding and more appreciative. We can tell she wants Jim to be less demanding when she says, "you tell me every day exactly what I should do and how I should do it. Do you think that just because you married me you own me?" We can tell that she wants him to be more appreciative when she says, "That is, if you can find someone who can stand to work for someone who is never satisfied."

Now, one final question about Ann and Jim: Given what we've seen of these two characters, do you think Ann will get her wish? Why or why not? Write your answer in the space below.

The most logical assumption is that Ann will probably not get her wish. Though this confrontation may open the door for future discussions that could help solve this couple's problems, the passage indicates that their problems are deeply rooted. One confrontation is not likely to lead to a resolution.

DETERMINING IMPLIED EFFECTS

In order to learn how to determine implied effects, take another look at Mr. Blank (the man who was robbed) and his building. Re-read the statements given by the building manager and Mr. Blank's neighbor and then use their statements to predict how the robbery will affect Mr. Blank and his building:

Building manager

This is the third robbery in our building this month. Each time, the thieves have gotten past building security with almost the entire contents of the victim's apartment. Yet each time, the security officers say they have seen nothing unusual.

Mr. Blank's neighbor

Well, Mr. Blank's a pretty carefree man. A few times I've knocked on his door and he just hollers, "Come in," and I just have to push the door open because it isn't locked. He often forgets things, too, like where he parked his car or where he put his keys. One time I found him in the hall searching through his bags because he couldn't find his keys, and it turned out the door was open anyway. Sometimes I wonder how he remembers to eat, let alone take care of his apartment.

Based on these two paragraphs, which of the following effects would be logical results (effects) of the robbery? Circle the correct answers.

1. Security will be tighter in the building from now on.

2. People moving furniture in and out of the building may be required to register with security.

3. The security officers will be fired.

4. Mr. Blank will get all of his belongings back.

5. Mr. Blank will be more careful about where he puts his keys.

6. Mr. Blank will get new locks on his door.

7. Mr. Blank will be sure to lock his door when he leaves.

8. Some tenants will leave the building.

Answers

Effects 1, 2, 5, 7, and 8 are logical predicted outcomes.

Effect 3 is not likely because it is too extreme; the building manager's statement does not suggest that he plans to fire the security guards. Rather, it suggests that he plans to look into the security problem.

There is nothing in either statement to suggest that effect 4 (that Mr. Blank will get his belongings back) is correct. In fact, there is no mention at all of his belongings.

Finally, because it is likely that Mr. Blank had left his door open on that day, there would be no need for him to get new locks on his door. Thus, number 6 is not a likely effect either.

SUMMARY

In reading, particularly in reading literature, as well as in real life, you often have to figure out what the causes of a particular event or situation might have been. The same is true of effects: both in reading and in life, you spend a lot of time trying to predict the outcomes of real or predicted actions or events. If you "read between the lines" without going too far beyond what the passage (or real-life event) actually contains, you can usually do a pretty good job of predicting these causes and effects.

Skill Building Until Next Time

- Observe people's behavior today. If you see people acting particularly happy, sad, or angry, or exhibiting some other strong emotion or behavior, see if you can find any clues as to the cause of their emotion or behavior. Are they reading a letter? Talking with someone? Waiting for something? *Why* are they reacting this way?
- Read a news article today that discusses a current event—an election, a train crash, or a political scandal, for example. What effects can you predict will come about as a result of this event? Try to come up with at least three predictions based on what you read.

L·E·S·S·O·N

EMOTIONAL VERSUS LOGICAL APPEALS

18

LESSON SUMMARY

Writers often appeal to your emotions to try to persuade you of something. But unless they also provide logical evidence to back up their claims, you have no *reason* to accept their argument as valid. This lesson helps you see how to distinguish between appeals to your emotions and appeals to your sense of reason.

Imagine that you are about to do something when someone runs up to you and says, "You can't do that!"

"Why not?" you ask.

"Because! You just can't, that's all."

Now, "Because!" is not likely to convince you that you shouldn't do what you were about to do, is it? Why not? Well, "Because!" does not provide you with a *reason* for not doing what you wanted to do. It is not, therefore, a very convincing argument.

> **Reason: a motive or justification for something; good sense or judgment**

While it is true that an appeal to emotions can help *strengthen* an argument based in logic, an argument cannot be valid if it is based solely on emotional appeal.

THE DIFFERENCE BETWEEN LOGICAL AND EMOTIONAL APPEALS

When writers—and others—want to convince people of something—to think or act in a certain way—they generally rely on two means of persuasion: appealing to the reader's sense of logic, and appealing to the reader's emotions. It is important to be able to distinguish between these two types of appeals because when writers rely *only* on appeals to emotion, they neglect to provide any real *evidence* for why you should believe what they say. Writers who rely solely on emotional appeals usually hope to get you so angry, or so scared, or so excited that you will forget to look for a sense of reason in their argument.

Unfortunately, many readers aren't aware of this strategy, so they may accept arguments that are weak and unfounded. People who use this emotional-appeals strategy are called *demagogues*—they try to win support by appealing to people's feelings and prejudices rather than to their sense of reason. Thus, you need to be able to look beyond these emotional appeals to determine if there is any *logic* behind them.

> **Logical: according to reason; according to conclusions drawn from evidence or good common sense**
> **Emotional: drawn from the emotions, from intense mental feelings**

DISTINGUISHING BETWEEN LOGICAL AND EMOTIONAL APPEALS

The best way to see the difference between logical and emotional appeals is to look at some examples. Actively read the passages that follow trying to discern whether the author is appealing primarily to your sense of reason or to your emotions.

PRACTICE PASSAGE 1

Start with the following passage. Read it carefully, marking it up as you go, and see if you can determine the author's strategy. Does he apppeal to your sense of logic, or only to your emotions? As you read, underline the reasons that the author provides for not wanting homosexuals to adopt children.

Homosexuals should not be allowed to adopt children. First of all, everyone knows that homosexuals are confused about their sexuality and that they don't know whether they're supposed to be men or women. If they don't know what they are, how are they supposed to teach their kids about sex? Their children will grow up confused about their sexuality, and they'll probably turn out to be homosexuals, too.

Second, homosexuals can't make babies naturally, so they can't possibly be good parents. If they can't have them the right way, then they shouldn't have them at all.

Furthermore, what if your child were friends with the child of a gay couple? Imagine how you would feel if your child came home after spending the night at his friend's house and told you his friend had two daddies. Why should your children have to be subjected to this perversity?

Chances are that no matter how you feel about homosexuality, this passage stirred up some pretty strong emotions. Perhaps you even found some of the writer's arguments convincing. But take another look at this passage. Is there any appeal to your sense of logic here—reason, evidence, or common sense? Or is the author appealing only to your emotions—your prejudices, fears, and uncertainties?

What Reasons Does the Writer Offer?

To help you see whether the writer's appeals are based on logic or emotion, break down his argument. The writer offers three different reasons for not wanting homosexual people to raise children. Can you list them below?

1.

2.

3.

You probably noticed that each of the three paragraphs deals with a different reason that homosexual people should not adopt children. They are:

1. Homosexual people are confused about their sexuality, so they will confuse their children, who will probably also turn out homosexual.

2. Homosexual people can't make babies naturally, so they can't be good parents.

3. Your child might become friends with the child of homosexual parents.

Are the Appeals Logical?

Now the next step is to see if these reasons are *logical.* Does the author come to these conclusions based on reason, evidence, or common sense? If you look carefully, you will see that the answer is no. Each of the writer's arguments is based purely on emotion without any logic to support it.

Begin with the first reason: *Homosexuals are confused about their sexuality, so they will confuse their children, who will probably also turn out to be homosexual.* Is there any logic behind this argument? Is this statement based on reason? Is there any evidence, such as statistics, that prove to us that all homosexual people are confused about their sexuality, or that their children will grow up confused about their sexuality, or that children of gay parents turn out to be gay themselves?

Regardless of whether you agree or disagree with this author, you can probably see that this argument is based only in emotion rather than logic. The argument crumbles when you break it down. The author tries to prevent you from looking behind his argument by saying that "everyone knows" homosexual people are confused about their sexuality. He states this as if it were a fact when, indeed, it is not. Even though you and many people you know may agree, no one can say with certainty that "everyone" knows this to be true—or whether it is true at all. In fact, some people may say that homosexual adults are not confused at all; they know that they are men or women who prefer the same gender. And if you cannot say for a fact that homosexual people are confused, then how can you say that they will confuse their children?

Even without this flaw, the writer's argument is not logical because there is no evidence in this essay that gay parents raise gay children. It may or may not be true; there's no way to tell from the author's argument, because he doesn't provide any evidence. People who think homosexual adults should be allowed to adopt children would counter that homosexuality is a lifestyle choice. They would point out that engineers don't always raise engineers, that police officers don't always raise police officers. There simply is no way to show that the author's argument is true even some of the time, much less *always*. Thus, this argument defies common sense.

The author's second argument is that *homosexuals can't make babies naturally, so they can't be good parents*. Is there any logic in this statement? No, there is not; this is an emotional appeal that addresses readers who don't think homosexuality is normal. These readers will be too busy agreeing with the writer to remember that there are many heterosexual parents who cannot have children naturally. Does that mean that heterosexual adults who can't have children naturally can't be good parents? No. And if those heterosexual people can be good parents, then the ability to bear children must not have anything to do with the quality of one's parenting. Thus, the argument is illogical.

The third argument is that *your children may become friends with the child of homosexual parents*. Of all of the reasons the author offers for homosexual people not adopting children, this most clearly plays upon readers' fears: "Imagine how you would feel," the author writes. But he doesn't tell you *why* this is wrong. Instead, he just calls it "perversity." Again, he avoids supporting his argument with logic, reason, or evidence.

PRACTICE PASSAGE 2

Now look at another argument on the same topic: whether homosexual people should be allowed to adopt children. Notice how much better this essay is—whether you agree with the author or not—simply because the author does not appeal solely to readers' emotions. Instead, her arguments are based in logic.

Homosexual people should be allowed to adopt children just like any other responsible adults. Although many people are against this idea, there is no reason that homosexual adults can't be just as good as parents as heterosexual people who adopt.

One of the biggest concerns people have is that the adopted children of homosexual people will grow up confused about their sexuality or that they will also turn out gay. But common sense tells us that the opposite is more likely to be true. Because homosexuals have been persecuted for so long, if they put any kind of pressure on their children regarding their sexuality, it will be pressure to be "normal" rather than gay. Why would they want their children to suffer in a prejudiced society? Furthermore, children of homosexual parents certainly cannot inherit homosexuality from their parents; after all, they are adopted.

Another argument is that homosexual people shouldn't have children because they can't have them naturally (and this apparently "proves" that homosexual people aren't "normal"). But there are hundreds of thousands of heterosexual couples who also can't have children naturally. Does that mean they're not normal? Does that mean they won't be good parents? Of course not. In fact, many times people who adopt are better parents because they don't take having children for granted. Good parents love their children—and natural birth is no prerequisite for love.

You probably noticed immediately that this passage is significantly longer than Practice Passage 1, even though this essay only gives us two reasons, whereas the first gave us three. It takes more time to write an argument that appeals to the reader's sense of logic than one that appeals to emotions alone.

What Reasons Does the Writer Offer?

Break this argument down as you did with the first one. Here are the reasons the author provides in arguing that homosexuals should be able to adopt children. Underneath each reason, write the *logic* behind the reason. What reasoning, evidence, or common sense does the author provide?

1. Children of homosexual parents will not necessarily be confused about their sexuality or turn out gay.

2. Homosexual people will be just as good as parents as heterosexual people.

Are the Appeals Logical?

Whether you agree with the author or not, you can see that this is a much more effective argument because the writer uses a sense of logic.

The first argument is supported by the following logic:

- Common sense tells us that homosexuals have suffered because of their lifestyle, so they wouldn't want their children to suffer the same. Thus, if they put any pressure on their children regarding their sexuality, it will be to be heterosexual, not homosexual.

- Adopted children of homosexuals can't inherit homosexuality.

The second argument is supported by the following logic:

- Heterosexuals can't always have children naturally, but that doesn't mean they can't be good parents. How someone acquires a child (through birth or adoption) does not determine how good or bad that parent will be.

MORE PRACTICE

Now that you've examined two brief essays—one that appeals to emotion and one that appeals to logic—see if you can correctly identify the approaches used by the writers of the following sentences. Look carefully for a sense of logic. If the writer is appealing to your emotions, is the author's argument also backed up by logic (common sense, reason, or evidence)? Write an E in the blank if it appeals *only* to your sense of emotion, and an L if it appeals to logic.

_____ **1.** Gun control is wrong, and anyone who tries to tell me that I can't own a gun is stupid.

_____ **2.** Gun control is wrong because it is a violation of our Constitutional right to bear arms.

_____ **3.** Every state should have capital punishment. If everyone knows that the penalty for certain crimes is death, people are much less likely to commit those crimes.

_____ **4.** We must have capital punishment. What if someone you love were killed; wouldn't you want the murderer to die?

_____ **5.** Capital punishment is wrong; if we kill someone who is guilty of murder, we are guilty of the same crime as the criminal.

Answers

It should be clear that argument 1 is an appeal to emotion without any logic and that arguments 2, 3, and 5 use common sense, evidence, and reason. But argument 4 may have confused you a bit. The argument may seem reasonable, but it does not address *why* the murderer should die rather than, say, spend a lifetime in jail. Most

of us might indeed wish death upon someone who murdered someone we love, but that is because we are deeply hurt by the loss of our loved one. Thus, this argument appeals to our emotions.

SUMMARY

Looking for appeals to logic will make you a more critical reader and thinker. And once you learn to read between the lines in an argument (to look behind emotional appeals for some sort of logical support), you'll have more confidence as a reader and be a better judge of the arguments that you hear and read.

Skill Building Until Next Time

- Listen carefully to how people around you try to convince you (or others) when they want you to think or act a certain way. For example, if a friend wants you to try a new place for lunch, how does he or she try to convince you: with appeals to your sense of logic ("The food is great—and so are the prices!") or to your emotions ("What, are you afraid to try something new?")? If your boss asks you to work overtime, does he or she appeal to your sense of logic ("You'll make lots of extra money") or to your emotions ("I could really, really use your help")? See which arguments you find most convincing and why.

- Read an editorial from the Opinion-Editorial page of your local newspaper. Look at how the writer supports his or her argument. Is the editiorial convincing? Why? What reasons or evidence does it use to support its position?

L·E·S·S·O·N

CRITICAL READING, CRITICAL THINKING

19

LESSON SUMMARY

You'll be introduced to a lot of different ideas and opinions when you read. This lesson introduces five components of *critical thinking* that will help you decide whether to accept what an author is saying.

n Lesson 18, you learned about the importance of distinguishing between emotional and logical appeals. When you looked for logical reasoning, you were using *critical reading* and *critical thinking* skills to assess the text. This skill—the ability to think critically about what you read—will take you to a new level of understanding and reading success.

Critical thinking means carefully and deliberately considering a claim or idea before you accept or reject it. There are five basic components of critical thinking. Some of them we've already discussed in previous lessons, so you already have some core critical thinking skills to build on. Critical thinking consists of:

- Considering the credibility of the author
- Distinguishing between fact and opinion
- Evaluating the evidence
- Looking out for "swayers"—subtly influential language
- Rejecting faulty reasoning

CONSIDER THE CREDIBILITY OF THE AUTHOR

Because *who* a writer is partially determines *what* he or she will say, critical readers and thinkers always ask questions about the writer. Who *is* the writer? How do I know he or she is an expert on the subject? Can I be reasonably comfortable that the facts the writer provides are true? To answer these questions, consider the writer's *expertise*. Expertise is determined by the author's:

- Education
- Accomplishments
- Reputation
- Position

For example, an author who is the head of a research institute, with a Ph.D. in psychology and 20 years of experience in dealing with patients, is probably a trustworthy author for an article about common causes of nervous breakdowns. A bank teller who had a nervous breakdown, however, is clearly not nearly as credible. Though she may have experienced a breakdown herself and may know, from her treatment, what caused her condition, she probably does not have the education, the accomplishments, the reputation, or the position to be considered a reliable expert on the general causes of nervous breakdowns. On the other hand, you'd rather read a description of the procedures for entering a deposit transaction by the bank teller than by the Ph.D. in psychology.

Furthermore, knowing something about the author's background gives you another advantage in critical reading and thinking: You can often tell whether you should be on the lookout for biases. A bias is an opinion or feeling that strongly favors one side of an argument. For example, if you know that the author of an editorial about capital punishment is also the parent of a murder victim, then you know that the author is probably going to be biased—he will probably have a very personal (and perhaps justifiable) desire to see murderers executed. But the author will still have to explain *why* convicted murderers should receive the death penalty rather than a life sentence. If you are aware of the author's biases (or potential for bias), then you can be sure to look extra hard for *logical* rather than just emotional support.

PRACTICE

1. The author of a book on parenting skills is described as a freelance writer living in Salt Lake City with her dog, Charlie. She has no children but works regularly with families at the community center. She has a master's degree in science education. How would you evaluate her credibility? If you do not think she's credible, what would make her more so? List your ideas below.

2. You are assigned several articles on the subject of whether violence on television affects the behavior of children. Rank the authors in order of whom you think has the most expertise on the subject (1 having the most expertise, 4 the least):

   _____ a member of the Board of Directors at NBC

   _____ a homemaker and mother of six children

_____a professor of sociology and author of a study on juvenile crime

_____a prominent child psychologist

3. Now rank those authors in order of who you think is the most unbiased of the authors (1 being the least biased, 4 the most biased).

Answers and Explanations

1. This author has a medium to low level of credibility. Though she has a master's degree, it is in _science_ education. She works with families at the community center, but that does not mean she has daily experience with children. The key to her low credibility is twofold: She is not a parent herself and she does not have an appropriate educational background. If her degree were in early childhood education or child psychology, or if she had children herself or we at least knew for sure that she worked with children daily, she would be much more credible.

2. **Expertise:** 3, 4, 1, 2. The professor who conducted a relevant study is probably the most credible expert on the subject, with the child psychologist (who might have read the professor's study) coming in second. The member of the Board of Directors may not have any children but probably is aware of studies and controversies related to television, so he's probably more credible than the homemaker.

3. **Bias:** 4, 3, 1, 2. The professor and the psychologist are probably equally unbiased. The homemaker ranks third with the member of the Board of Directors as the most biased. The board member certainly has something at stake here, so he will strongly favor one side of the argument.

DISTINGUISH BETWEEN FACT AND OPINION

Lesson 4 talked about one of the basics of reading comprehension: distinguishing between **fact** and **opinion**. Remember that facts are things _known_ for certain to have happened, to be true, or to exist. Opinions, on the other hand, are things _believed_ to have happened, to be true, or to exist. Critical reading and thinking hinges on knowing and recognizing this difference.

When writers provide facts, we can generally accept them, so long as we believe the author to be credible. But opinions are a different story. Critical thinkers don't simply accept opinions. When they come across an opinion, they look for logical support for that opinion and _then_ decide whether or not to accept it.

PRACTICE

Indicate whether each of the following is a fact (F) or an opinion (O).

_____Meat grilled over hickory coals tastes better than meat grilled over mesquite.

_____Meat grilled over hickory coals tastes different from meat grilled over mesquite.

_____Steven Spielberg's latest movie stars Harrison Ford and Nicole Kidman.

_____Steven Spielberg's latest movie is his best so far.

Answers

O, F, F, O. If you answered any of these incorrectly, please go back and review Lesson 4 carefully.

EVALUATE THE EVIDENCE

Facts don't need supporting evidence; they *are* evidence. But when you come across an opinion, look for supporting evidence. What makes Spielberg's latest movie his best so far? Is it the riveting plot? The cinematography and special effects? The incredible suspense? Is it because the leading man is your favorite actor? Or because you love monster movies?

Obviously some of these reasons are more logical (and therefore offer stronger support) than others. Your task as a critical thinker is to see first of all if there *is* any evidence, and then to evaluate the *strength* of that evidence. As you learned in Lesson 18, the more logical the evidence or support, the better. Opinions supported by opinions aren't very effective because there's no reason for a reader to share the author's opinion.

PRACTICE

Fill in the following blanks to form an *opinion*, and then provide support for your opinion. Try to supply at least three *logical* reasons for each in the spaces provided.

1. _____ (*the last movie you saw*) is
   _____ .

2. Capital punishment (*or any other issue, like abortion or euthanasia*)

   _____

   _____ .

Possible Answers

Be sure that you formed opinions—debatable responses that you believe to be true but with which others may disagree.

1. A possible answer here is: "*The Peacemaker* is an exciting but unrealistic movie." Be sure you provided logical support for your opinion.

2. One possible answer goes like this: "Capital punishment should be enforced nationwide. It is likely to reduce the number of violent crimes. It metes out appropriate justice—an eye for eye. If you kill somebody (except in self-defense), you should also suffer the same fate. And it will save taxpayers money."

LOOK OUT FOR "SWAYERS"

As you learned in Lesson 12, the words a writer chooses can have a powerful effect on the reader. By carefully choosing their words, writers can often influence or "sway" you in a certain direction without you realizing it. Three common ways authors sway readers are through *euphemisms*, *dysphemisms*, and *loaded questions*.

Euphemisms

When a writer substitutes a neutral or positive word or phrase for a negative one, that's a *euphemism*. To say someone "passed on," for example, is a euphemism for saying someone died. A euphemism is a tricky way to sway you emotionally. For example, a writer who believes that war is good might call war a "military exercise." This phrase clearly takes away the negative connotations of death and violence that the word "war" conveys.

Dysphemisms

Dysphemisms are the opposite of euphemisms: The writer substitutes a negative word or phrase for a positive or neutral one. For example, if someone calls a psychiatrist a "shrink," that's a dysphemism. Similarly, to call euthanasia "murder" is a dysphemism. Even if the author believes that euthanasia is murder, the two terms are not interchangeable. But "murder" clearly conveys how the writer feels about euthanasia, and the writer is clearly trying to make you feel that way, too.

Loaded Questions

Loaded questions push you toward a certain answer rather than being fair and open. Look at the difference in these two questions:

1. Would you support a bill that legalized euthanasia?

2. Would you support a bill that allowed doctors to murder their terminally ill patients?

The way question 2 is worded makes it hard for you to answer "yes" to the question; if you answer "yes," it would seem like you're supporting the murder of patients. But question 1 is fair—you can answer "yes" or "no" without seeming like you support murder.

PRACTICE

Determine whether the following sentences contain a euphemism (E), dysphemism (D), loaded question (L), or none of the above (N).

1. All influence peddlers should be banned from Capitol Hill.

2. Should condoms be distributed to students in public high schools?

3. He used some creative accounting methods to cover up the error.

4. Should we promote premarital sex by distributing condoms to high school students?

Answers

1. (D) Dysphemism, substituting "influence peddlers" for "lobbyists."
2. (N) None. This is a fair question.
3. (E) Euphemism, substituting "creative accounting methods" for "manipulated the numbers" or a similar phrase.
4. (L) Loaded question. If you answer yes, you seem to be supporting premarital sex among high school students.

REJECT FAULTY REASONING

Much of what is generally considered faulty reasoning is simply emotional appeal rather than logical reasoning. Writers often fall back on emotional "reasoning" when they lack logical support for their argument. They may also try to pass off what looks like logical reasoning but in reality is not. There are many different types of this false reasoning, also called *pseudoreasoning*. Five of the most common are discussed here.

Red Herring/Smokescreen

In this type of pseudoreasoning, the writer distracts your attention from the issue by bringing in another, irrelevant topic. People often use red herrings when they're afraid you'll see that they don't really have support for their argument. The idea is to get you thinking about something else so that you don't come back and question them on the original issue. For example:

> A tax increase is necessary. After all, look at how little our children are learning in our public schools.

While the quality of public education is an important issue, it doesn't seem to have anything to do with why a tax increase is necessary. Of course, federal funds do go to public education, but the connection between the two issues must be clear. Here it is not, and we risk ending up in a debate about education, not about taxes.

Ad Hominem

Ad hominem is Latin for *to the man*. This type of pseudoreasoning happens when the writer attacks a person or group of people instead of an idea. In essence, it argues that you should reject an idea because of who said it, not because the idea is good or bad. For example:

> Don't believe him. He's a Republican.
> Kate said that? Then it can't be true.

Slippery Slope

Sometimes writers will use the *slippery slope* "argument" to get you to reject an idea. They suggest that if A happens, it will lead to B, then C, and then . . . disaster. It's the "next thing you know" argument. For example:

> If we legalize marijuana, next thing you know they'll legalize cocaine and heroin too—and we'll be a nation of drug addicts.

Non Sequitur

When a writer jumps to conclusions, he's committing the error in reasoning known as a *non sequitur* (meaning *it doesn't follow*). The writer is making a hasty generalization—coming to a conclusion too quickly. Just because A is true doesn't mean B is true. For example:

> On the second day of class, a teacher thinks, "She didn't do her homework. She's irresponsible."

If that student continues not to do her homework, then perhaps the teacher's conclusion is justified. But to come to that conclusion after only one incident is unfair. Perhaps the student didn't understand the assignment; perhaps she was ill; perhaps . . . there are endless possibilities. The point is that her teacher jumped to a conclusion.

Post Hoc, Ergo Propter Hoc

Post hoc, ergo propter hoc is also Latin; it means *after this, therefore because of this*. This error in reasoning occurs when we assume that just because A came before B, A *caused* B. For example:

> Margot got into a fight with her roommate this morning. That's why she decided to move out.

The fight with her roommate may be the reason, or a reason, why Margot decided to move out. But this type of reasoning doesn't take into consideration other possible causes—and there are probably many. Maybe Margot never got along with her roommate, and this was just one of many fights. Maybe she got a new job and has to relocate. Maybe she's wanted to live alone for a while and can finally afford to do so.

If you're having trouble with these ideas, you may want to review Lesson 9, which looks at cause and effect in writing.

PRACTICE

Decide what type of faulty reasoning is used in the sentences below.

1. Don't listen to what he says about relationships. He just got divorced again.

2. I don't think "three strikes and you're out" for convicted felons is a good policy. Next thing you know it will be two strikes, and then one. Then we'll be sticking people in jail for life for misdemeanors.

3. Violent crime in this state skyrocketed after the Brady Bill went into effect. The bill that was supposed to *reduce* violent crime actually *increased* it!

4. Wow. The first day of class was really boring. This is going to be a looong semester!

5. I did not accept any illegal campaign contributions. But speaking of illegal and immoral, look at what my opponent is planning to do to welfare in this state.

Answers

1. *Ad hominem.* The writer wants you to refuse to listen because of who is speaking—someone who just got divorced—not because what he says is invalid.

2. Slippery slope. A three-strikes policy is not likely to lead to a one-strike policy.

3. *Post hoc, ergo propter hoc.* There could be dozens of reasons for the increase in violent crime.

4. *Non sequitur.* The first class isn't necessarily an indication of how the class will go for the rest of the semester. Besides, it's difficult to delve into material on the first day because the class roster is usually still unsettled.

5. Red herring. The writer is trying to distract you from his campaign funding by focusing your attention on his opponent.

SUMMARY

As a college student, you need to be able to *assess* what you read as well as *understand* it. Critical thinking skills enable you to make wise judgments about what you read. By considering the credibility of the author; distinguishing between fact and opinion; and looking for evidence, swayers, and faulty reasoning, you can determine whether you should accept ideas and opinions or reject them—or suspend your judgment until you can learn more about the issue.

Skill Building Until Next Time

- Listen to a talk show on the radio. This is a good place to hear a lot of faulty reasoning and swayers. You will also have the chance to assess the credibility of speakers and the logic of their arguments.
- Read an editorial or letter to the editor in your local paper, preferably one that gives some information about the author's background. How do you assess the credibility of the author? Can you find any swayers or faulty reasoning? Can you distinguish between fact and opinion?

L·E·S·S·O·N 20

FINDING MEANING IN LITERATURE

LESSON SUMMARY

Lots of people are scared of reading literature—stories, poems, and plays—especially if they have to answer questions about it, as in a classroom or test situation. But now that you know so much about finding an implied main idea, you can also find the *theme,* or main idea, of a work of literature. This lesson works with poetry to show you how to do it.

O h no! Not the "L" word!

Yes, it's time to talk about *literature.* Like many people, you may be intimidated by this ten-letter word. This is quite natural; after all, in literature (novels, poems, stories, and plays), the writers don't come right out and tell us what they mean. But, just as you were able to find the implied main idea in a passage where there was no topic sentence, you can look for clues the author has left behind to find the *theme* (the main idea) in any work of literature. You simply need to read between the lines to find meaning.

You probably remember the word *theme* from your high school English courses. Maybe you remember it with some confusion and trepidation. It's not as complicated as you might think.

You've spent a lot of time finding the main idea of a piece of writing. Finding the theme of a work of literature is similar to finding the main idea of a paragraph. Just as a main idea is more than the *subject* of a paragraph or passage, the theme of a work of literature is also more than just its subject: It is what the text says *about* that subject. Theme, in other words, is the overall message or idea that a work of literature conveys. For example, you can probably figure out from the title that the *subject* of John Donne's poem "Death Be Not Proud" is death. However, the *theme* is not merely "death," but what the poem says *about* death, which happens to be that death is a gift if one believes in God.

There isn't room in this short lesson to look at theme in a short story, novel, or play. So this lesson will introduce you to a few poems. But don't be frightened: Reading poetry is really just like reading anything else. You just have to read a little more carefully and rely a little more on your sense of observation. You find theme in poetry the same way you do in other kinds of writing: by looking for clues in what happens and in the words the writer uses to describe what happens.

How Action Conveys Theme

First, look at an example of how the action of a poem—what happens in it—leads you to understand the theme.

PRACTICE PASSAGE 1

Read the following poem by William Blake from his book *Songs of Experience*, published in 1794. Read it out loud, because poetry is meant to be *heard* as well as read. Then read it again with your pen in hand: Read actively, making your observations and comments in the margins. Then answer the questions that follow.

A Poison Tree

I was angry with my friend;
I told my wrath, my wrath did end.   *wrath = anger*
I was angry with my foe: *foe = enemy*
I told it not, my wrath did grow.

And I water'd it in fears,
Night & morning with my tears;
And I sunned it with smiles,
And with soft deceitful wiles.   *wiles = trickery, deceit*

And it grew both day and night,
Till it bore an apple bright;
And my foe beheld it shine,
And he knew that it was mine.

And into my garden stole
When the night had veil'd the pole: *veiled = concealed*
In the morning glad I see
My foe outstretch'd beneath the tree.

What Happened?

To understand the author's theme, you need to look carefully at what happened, and why. Look at each of the four stanzas (a stanza is a poetic "paragraph"; each stanza in this poem is four lines long) to track the action.

What happens in the first stanza?

1. The speaker was angry with
   a. a friend
   b. a foe
   c. his friend and his foe

2. How did the speaker handle his anger toward his friend?

   a. He told his friend about it and it went away.

   b. He kept it to himself and it grew.

   c. He kept it to himself and it went away.

3. How did the speaker handle his anger toward his foe?

   a. He told his friend about it and it went away.

   b. He kept it to himself and it grew.

   c. He kept it to himself and it went away.

You probably figured out the answers without too much trouble: **1. c, 2. a, 3. b.**

Now look at the scond stanza. The key to understanding this stanza is knowing what "it" refers to. Reread the first and second stanzas carefully in order to answer the next question.

4. "It" refers to

   a. tears

   b. smiles

   c. wrath

"Wrath" is the last thing mentioned in the first stanza, so it follows that "wrath" is what "it" refers to.

The second stanza tells us that the speaker "water'd" it (his wrath) with fears and "sunned" it with smiles and wiles. How can this be? Can you literally water and sun your anger? No, but the speaker is not being literal here. Instead, he is using figurative language. Like the similes we saw earlier about Mr. B, comparing his eyes to knives and his mustache to Hitler's, this stanza uses a *metaphor*—a comparison that doesn't use the words *like* or *as*—to compare the speaker's wrath to something that grows with water and sun. Now, given these clues (and the best clue of all, the title of the

poem), to what exactly is the speaker comparing his wrath?

5. The speaker compares his wrath to

   a. a flower

   b. a tree

   c. the sun

The answer, of course, is **b**, a tree. The title gives this away. Also, a tree is the only plant that could bear "an apple bright," as in the third stanza.

What else happens in the third stanza?

6. In the third stanza, the foe

   a. grows his own apple

   b. shines the speaker's apple

   c. sees the speaker's apple

The answer is **c**, the foe sees the speaker's apple ("my foe beheld it shine").

Finally, what happens in the fourth stanza? This stanza is somewhat trickier than the others, because in this stanza, something happens that is not directly stated. You know that the foe sneaks into the speaker's garden ("And into my garden stole"), but what else happens?

The poem doesn't exactly tell you, but you can guess. The speaker had an apple; you know that this apple grew on a tree and that this tree is a metaphor for the speaker's anger. You also know that the poem is called "A Poison Tree." You read in the fourth stanza that, in the morning, the speaker finds his foe "outstretch'd beneath the tree." What can you conclude?

7. At the end of the fourth stanza, the foe
   a. is waiting to ambush the speaker and kill him with the apple
   b. has been killed by the apple he stole because it was poisonous
   c. is waiting to share the apple with the speaker

Which answer do your clues add up to? The only one that can be correct is **b**. The speaker was angry; the tree (and so the apple) was poisonous. You know that the foe, seeing the apple, snuck into the speaker's garden. Apparently he ate the apple, because now he's "outstretch'd beneath the tree." You also know that the speaker is "glad" to see his foe outstretched this way—he's glad to see him dead.

What Does It Mean?

Okay, so that's what happened in the poem. But what does it all mean?

Look again at the action. What the speaker *did* was to tell his friend about his wrath. What the speaker *didn't* do was to tell his enemy about his wrath. The results of the speaker's action and his inaction are your clues to the meaning of the poem as a whole, its theme.

8. Which of the following best summarizes the theme of the poem?
   a. Don't steal; it can kill you.
   b. Choose your enemies carefully.
   c. If you don't talk about your anger, it can be deadly.

Before you go any further, think about your answer again. Like a main idea, a theme must be general enough to encompass the whole work, not just a piece of it. Does the answer you chose encompass the whole poem and not just part of it?

You should have chosen answer **c**, for this is the idea that sums up the message or "lesson" of the poem. In the first two lines, the speaker's wrath for his friend vanished when he talked about it, but he did not talk about his wrath for his enemy. Instead, he let it grow until it was poisonous and deadly.

HOW LANGUAGE CONVEYS EMOTION

In addition to conveying a theme, poems also often use language to create a powerful image or emotion. After looking at how poets use language to convey an emotion or a picture, you'll be ready to put your understanding of the action and the language together to understand the meaning of a poem.

PRACTICE PASSAGE 2

Take a look at the following poem by the British poet Alfred, Lord Tennyson, as an example of how language can convey a strong feeling by conveying an image or picture. Read "The Eagle" twice out loud—remember, poetry is meant to be heard, not just seen. Then mark it up and write your observations in the margin.

The Eagle

He clasps the crag with crooked hands;   *crag = steep*
Close to the sun in lonely lands,   *or rugged rock*
Ringed with the azure world, he stands.   *azure =*
   sky blue

The wrinkled sea beneath him crawls;
He watches from his mountain walls,
And like a thunderbolt he falls.

The Sound of Words

What did you notice about the language in this poem? Did you notice the rhyme in each stanza—*hands, lands, stands* and *crawls, walls, falls*? Did you notice the repetition of the "k" sound in *clasp, crag,* and *crooked*? This repetition of sounds (especially at the beginning of words) is called *alliteration.*

9. Which other line of this poem uses alliteration?
   a. line 2
   b. line 3
   c. line 6

The answer is line 2, which repeats the *l* sound in "*lonely lands.*"

Picture Language

You may have noticed another poetic device at work in this poem. In line 1, the poet tells us that the eagle ("he") "clasps" the rock "with crooked hands." Do eagles have hands? No, they do not; but Tennyson gives the eagle human characteristics. When an animal is given human characteristics, or when a inanimate thing (like a rock, for example) is given animate characteristics (human or animal), it is called *personification.*

10. Which other line of this poem uses personification?
   a. line 2
   b. line 4
   c. line 6

The other example of personification is found in line 4, where the sea "crawls" like a baby or a turtle.

Here's a memory test:

11. Line 6, "And like a thunderbolt he falls," uses which of the following poetic devices?
   a. personification
   b. simile
   c. irony

This line uses **b**, a simile that compares the eagle to a thunderbolt. What is the effect of this comparison?

12. The comparison of the eagle to a thunderbolt makes the reader think of the eagle as
   a. a weak, timid creature
   b. an unpredictable creature
   c. a powerful, fast creature

Like all good similes, this comparison creates a vivid image that not only helps us actually picture the eagle's flight but also tells us *something about* the eagle by comparing it to the incredible force of nature that is lightning. The eagle, this simile suggests, is as powerful, as fast, as dangerous—and as impossible to catch—as a thunderbolt. We should, in short, be as awed by the eagle as we are by lightning—and that feeling, more than an idea we might call a theme, is what this poem is all about.

ACTION + LANGUAGE = THEME

In the final poem for today, by the American poet Stephen Crane, see if you can determine the theme of the poem by looking at both the action of the poem and its language (diction, style, and tone). As before, begin by reading the poem carefully, first out loud and then with pen in hand.

PRACTICE PASSAGE 3

A Man Said to the Universe

A man said to the universe:
"Sir, I exist!"
"However," replied the universe,
"The fact has not created in me
A sense of obligation."

13. Which sentence best summarizes the theme of this poem?
    a. The universe is too big for humanity.
    b. The universe is indifferent to humanity.
    c. Humanity has an obligation to the universe.

The best answer is **b**, "The universe is indifferent to humanity." This idea is conveyed in part by the action of the poem: what the man says to the universe and the universe's reply. But the universe's indifference is also reflected in the language of the poem.

14. Which of the following best describes the tone of this poem?
    a. warm, caring
    b. hot, angry
    c. cold, formal

The words of this poem—especially "sir," "fact," and "sense of obligation"—are cold, formal words that reflect the way the universe feels about man: indifferent. There is no sense of intimacy, no relationship, no warmth in these words. The poet's diction and style help to reveal the theme of the poem.

SUMMARY

Reading poetry wasn't so bad after all, was it? If you are an active reader who is sensitive to the language used by the poet, you can use the clues the poet gives you to help you enjoy the pictures and emotions created through words and understand the poem's theme. And if you can do this for poems, you can certainly do it for stories, novels, and plays as well.

Skill Building Until Next Time

- Read a poem on your own today. See if you can read between the lines to determine its theme.
- Read a short story today. Apply the techniques you used to determine the theme in a poem to determine the theme of the story.

L·E·S·S·O·N

READING ACROSS THE CURRICULUM

LESSON SUMMARY

Each academic discipline has its own approach to research, teaching, and writing. By being aware of what the different disciplines write about and *how* they write about those subjects, you can dramatically improve your reading comprehension across the curriculum.

Now that you have some strategies for making sense of literature, you're ready to tackle other subjects. Reading across the curriculum, that is, reading in various subjects or disciplines, is not as daunting as it may sound. If you are aware of the *conventions* of the different disciplines, you'll understand much more of what you read. Conventions are like rules for different kinds of reading and writing; each discipline does things a little differently. That's why the most important thing you can do to prepare to read texts for subjects as diverse as psychology, English, and physics is to know what questions to ask. Most academic disciplines can be grouped into three larger categories:

- **Humanities,** including literature, philosophy, art, religion
- **Natural sciences,** including biology, physics, chemistry
- **Social sciences,** including history, psychology, sociology, economics

You learned some tips for dealing with literature in the previous lesson. In this lesson, you'll look at reading strategies for other subjects in the humanities as well as in the natural sciences and social sciences. We'll start with the sciences because the strategies you learn there will be helpful in the other disciplines.

READING IN THE NATURAL SCIENCES

Many people think of scientific writing as the "opposite" of literary writing. That's because when you read literature, you often have to look for subtle clues to the meaning, or theme, of the text. You have to pay particular attention to the language the writer uses and draw conclusions from your observations. Scientific texts, on the other hand, aim to make their language and ideas as clear and unambiguous as possible. Meaning is explicit, not implied, and you generally find few similes or metaphors. So scientific texts should be easy to read, right?

Well, not necessarily. While you may not have to "read between the lines" to find meaning, scientific texts pose a different challenge. They tend to rely heavily on specific, technical vocabulary (*jargon*), and they tend to be loaded with facts. These characteristics often present difficulties for readers.

Scientific texts become much more manageable if you approach them with the following strategies:

- Ask the right questions
- Pay attention to vocabulary
- Take good notes
- Take it one step at a time
- Make connections

ASK THE RIGHT QUESTIONS

Most scientific texts aim to **explain** natural phenomena or the results of observations or experiments. They also usually indicate *why* the information they provide is important—how it affects us or how it fits into a larger picture and relates to other facts and phenomena.

If the text you're reading is describing an experiment or procedure—that is, if it aims to explain how or why something happens or happened, like how a liquid turns into a gas—then the following questions can help you better understand the material:

- What happens/happened?
- How does/did it happen?
- Why does/did it happen (that way)?
- Why is this important?

On the other hand, if the text is describing some*thing*—that is, if it aims to explain what something is or does—then the following questions will be more helpful:

- What is X?
- What does it do?
- How does it do it?
- Why is it important?

Notice that both sets of questions use the same key question words: *what*, *how*, and *why*. And both sets include the critical question, "Why is it important?" That's because all of the information in scientific texts exist in a *context*—in relationship to other things—and you need to understand that relationship.

PAY ATTENTION TO VOCABULARY

Be sure to look up and write down the meaning of any unfamiliar words—and even familiar words if they are used in a scientific sense. That is, you may already know what a word like *light* means in the common sense, but you may also be expected to know its specific *scientific* definition.

TAKE GOOD NOTES

Because scientific texts are laden with facts—facts that often build on each other—it is important that you take good notes. Keep track of key concepts and *summarize* frequently, section by section or even paragraph by paragraph. And give examples of key concepts; this will make those concepts easier to remember.

TAKE IT ONE STEP AT A TIME

When it doubt, take it one sentence (or one phrase) at a time. As soon as you find yourself getting lost, stop and go back. It's better to take twice as long and come out understanding the material than to finish quickly without comprehension.

MAKE CONNECTIONS

Again, because scientific texts are so loaded with facts, it's important to note exactly how those facts fit together. You can do this with words, or you can use pictures and diagrams. Consider how the phenomenon you are reading about relates to other phenomena, how it is important in your life, or how it affects the world around you.

PRACTICE

Read the following passage about the immune system actively and carefully, employing the strategies above. Take good notes and then answer the questions that follow. Use your own words in your answers as much as possible.

The immune system, which protects the body from infections, diseases, and other injuries, is composed of the lymphatic system and the skin. Lymph nodes, which measure about 1 to 25 centimeters across, and small vessels called lymphatics compose the lymphatic system. The nodes are located in the groin, armpits, throat, and trunk and are connected by the lymphatics. White blood cells in the nodes attack and ingest infectious agents like bacteria and fungus. When battling infection, the lymph nodes are often swollen and sensitive.

The skin, the largest organ of the human body, is also considered part of the immune system. Hundreds of small nerves in the skin send messages to the brain to communicate pressure, pain, and other sensations. The skin encloses the organs to prevent injuries and forms a protective barrier that repels dirt and water and stops the entry of most harmful chemicals. Sweat glands in the skin help regulate the body's temperature, and other glands release oils that can kill or impede the growth of certain bacteria. Hair follicles in the skin also provide protection, especially of the skull and groin.

1. What is the immune system?

2. What does it do?

3. How does it do it?

4. Why is it important?

Answers

The next page shows how you might have taken notes for this passage and answered the questions.

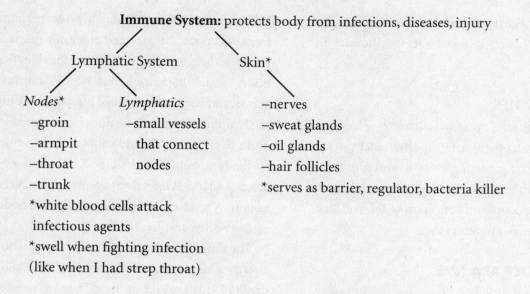

Immune System: protects body from infections, diseases, injury

Lymphatic System   Skin*

*Nodes**   *Lymphatics*   —nerves
–groin   –small vessels   –sweat glands
–armpit   that connect   –oil glands
–throat   nodes   –hair follicles
–trunk   *serves as barrier, regulator, bacteria killer
*white blood cells attack
 infectious agents
*swell when fighting infection
(like when I had strep throat)

1. The immune system is made up of the *lymphatic system* (*lymph nodes* located in the groin, armpits, throat, and trunk, connected by vessels called *lymphatics*) and the *skin.*
2. The immune system protects us from infections, diseases, and injuries.
3. The skin protects the body by covering it like an envelope and keeping out dirt, water, and chemicals. Nerves in the skin send signals to the brain when they feel pressure or pain. Sweat glands help regulate body temperature, and other glands in the skin produce bacteria-killing oils. Hair follicles also form a barrier. White blood cells in the lymph nodes attack and ingest bacteria and other infectious agents.
4. The immune system is essential for protecting our bodies from harm and keeping them free from disease and infection.

READING IN THE SOCIAL SCIENCES

Like biology, physics, chemistry, and the other physical and natural sciences, each of the disciplines within the social sciences has its own jargon. So once again it is important to look up any unfamiliar words. And, like texts in the sciences, those in the social science are often loaded with facts. This means that taking good notes and making connections are also important. Thus, the same five steps you learned for reading in the natural sciences are also important in the social sciences.

With the social sciences, there's also the added challenge of dealing with theories and opinions. That's because social science texts generally try to explain *people* and their behaviors rather than natural or physical phenomena. Because people do not behave according to fixed natural or physical laws, many conclusions in the social sciences are interpretive—and therefore debatable. As a result, in the social sciences, you need to ask a slightly different set of questions.

For texts that describe events or experiments (historical events, for example, or a psychological experiment), ask:

- What happens/happened?
- When does/did it happen?
- Why does/did it happen (that way)?
- What is/was the result?
- Why is/was this important?
- *How credible is the author?*
- *What evidence does the author offer?*
- *How logical are the author's conclusions?*

For texts that describe a concept, theory, or principle (like supply and demand or Pavlovian conditioning, for example), ask:

- What is the concept, theory, or principle?
- How does it work?
- Why does it work this way?
- Why is it important?
- *How credible is the author?*
- *What evidence does the author offer?*
- *How logical are the author's conclusions?*

CONTROVERSY IN THE SOCIAL SCIENCES

We must ask the last three questions above because much in the social sciences is highly interpretive. As a result, there are often many theories or ideas about the same thing. The atomic bombing of Hiroshima, Japan, is a perfect example. More than 50 years after World War II, there is still a great deal of controversy not only over whether or not we should have dropped the bomb, but also *why* we dropped the bomb. (Some say it was for political, not military, reasons.) For example, an account of the bombing told by a university history professor may be quite different from the account told by an official military historian. And both accounts may be quite

different from that told by a Japanese historian. History, just like any other social science, is subject to interpretation. *What* happened may be clear, but *why* it happened is often debatable. Be sure to use your critical thinking skills to help you decide which account is most credible. (Review Lesson 19 for a reminder of how to evaluate authors' credibility.)

Not all of the social science texts you read will be so openly controversial, of course, and much of your reading will probably be from textbooks that summarize the major concepts and theories in the field. Of course, you will also be expected to remember certain dates and facts that are *not* disputable. Whatever the topic, remember the strategies for reading across the curriculum, and don't forget to read actively and think critically about what you read.

PRACTICE

Below is a short passage from the first chapter of Sigmund Freud's *Beyond the Pleasure Principle*, published in 1920. In it, Freud explains some of the characteristics of the *pleasure principle:* the underlying human drive to avoid "unpleasure" and seek pleasure at all times. Read the following passage carefully and actively, using the social sciences reading strategies, and then answer the questions that follow.

It must be pointed out…that strictly speaking it is incorrect to talk of the dominance of the pleasure principle over the course of mental processes. If such a dominance existed, the immense majority of our mental processes would have to be accompanied by pleasure or lead to pleasure, whereas universal experience completely contradicts any such conclusion. The most that can be said, therefore, is that there exists in the mind a strong *tendency* towards the pleasure principle, but that that tendency is opposed by certain other forces or circumstances, so that the final outcome cannot always be in harmony with the tendency towards pleasure….

The first example of the pleasure principle being inhibited in this way is a familiar one which occurs with regularity. We know that the pleasure principle is proper to a *primary* method of working on the part of the mental apparatus, but that, from the point of view of the self-preservation of the organism among the difficulties of the external world, it is from the very outset inefficient and even highly dangerous. Under the influence of the ego's instincts of self-preservation, the pleasure principle is replaced by the *reality principle*. This latter principle does not abandon the intention of ultimately obtaining pleasure, but it nevertheless demands and carries into effect the postponement of satisfaction, the abandonment of a number of possibilities of gaining satisfaction and the temporary toleration of unpleasure—a step on the long indirect road to pleasure.

1. Why are we not completely controlled by the pleasure principle?

2. What evidence does Freud give that the pleasure principle can be dangerous?

3. What counteracts the pleasure principle?

4. Why are the ideas Freud poses here important?

5. Does this seem like a valid theory to you? Why or why not?

Answers

1. If the pleasure principle controlled all of our actions, it could be inefficient and even deadly.

2. [You might have answered something like this:] Well, he doesn't in this passage, but I can think of several examples. Drug addicts, for example, allow themselves to be ruled by the pleasure principle,

which goes contrary to the instinct of self-preservation and can lead to severe illness and death.

3. The reality principle counteracts the pleasure principle.

4. Freud's notion is that we are driven by our desire to seek pleasure and avoid pain. This is a theory that explains most of our behaviors.

5. [You might have answered something like this:] Yes. Freud doesn't give any examples here, but the concept makes sense; I myself take actions that may not give me immediate pleasure (like taking a math class, for example), but I know in the long run I'll gain pleasure out of it (I'll get a degree and a job, etc.). Some of us live more by the pleasure principle and less by the reality principle than others.

READING IN THE HUMANITIES

You learned strategies for reading literature in Lesson 20, but there are several other subjects in the humanities that you'll likely be required to study—philosophy, religion, art, or music, for example. Texts in the humanities often express ideas about the nature of existence or thought, about spirituality, or about the visual or performing arts.

In the humanities, as in the social sciences, you'll probably spend most of your time reading from texts that summarize major concepts and theories. However, you may on occasion read *primary texts*—that is, the texts that originally proposed those ideas—and you will often be asked to look at *criticism*. For example, you may, in an art history class, study a certain artist and read what critics have said about his or her work. When you come across such criticism, one of the best things you can do to improve your comprehension is to use your critical thinking skills. In particular, you should be sure to *look for evidence: why* does the author say X about Y?

Though texts in the humanities range considerably in subject matter and level of difficulty, several questions should help your reading comprehension in subjects besides literature. Keep in mind the same reading strategies you used for the other disciplines, and ask yourself:

■ When was this written? (When dealing with ideas like those in the humanities, the social, political, and religious *contexts* of the time in which the text was written are very important.)
■ What does the author believe to be true?
■ Why does the author believe this to be true?
■ Why is this important?

PRACTICE

Below is a short passage from "Essay II—Of Suicide" by the eighteenth-century English philosopher David Hume. Keep in mind the following context: Hume wrote this at a time when the church was very powerful in England, and it was the church's position that suicide is a sin. Read the passage actively and carefully and then answer the questions that follow:

Were the disposal of human life so much reserved as the peculiar province of the almighty that it were an encroachment on his right for men to dispose of their own lives; it would be equally criminal to act for the preservation of life as for its destruction. If I turn aside a stone which is falling upon my head, I disturb the course of nature, and I invade the peculiar province of the almighty by lengthening out my life beyond the period which by the general laws of matter and motion he had assigned to it.

....

It would be no crime in me to divert the *Nile* or *Danube* from its course, were I able to effect such purposes. Where then is the crime of turning a few ounces of blood from their natural channel?

1. How does Hume feel about suicide?

2. Why?

3. Why do you think this text is important?

4. What do you think of Hume's argument?

Answers

1. Clearly, Hume does not feel that suicide is a sin. Rather, he feels that man's ability to take his own life is in keeping with the natural laws that God created, and it is as natural to end one's life as it is to prolong or preserve it.

2. Hume's main argument here is that if it is not a sin to "disturb the course of nature" to preserve one's life, then it should not be considered a sin to end one's life.

3. It was clearly a text that clashed with the predominant beliefs of the time. Also, by this argument, Hume gives humans much more power over their own destiny. (Rather than leaving our death in God's hands, we can take it into our own hands—without offending God.) In addition, Hume's arguments are important since they relate to present-day controversial issues like euthanasia.

4. Answers, of course, will vary.

SUMMARY

Whether you're reading about physics or political science, it is important to ask the right questions, take good notes, pay attention to vocabulary, and otherwise read actively and critically. Following these reading strategies will help you understand more of what you read across the curriculum.

Skill Building Until Next Time

- Employ the reading strategies covered in this lesson in the work that you do for other classes this week.
- Share some of these reading strategies with a friend. Explaining them to someone else will help you remember them better.

L·E·S·S·O·N
22
DRAWING CONCLUSIONS: PUTTING IT ALL TOGETHER

LESSON SUMMARY

This lesson wraps up your study of reading comprehension by reviewing everything you've learned so far.

Y ou're almost at the end of this book. If you've been doing a lesson every weekday, you've spent a month building your reading skills. Congratulations! This lesson uses a longer passage than the ones you've read so far to give you a chance to practice all the skills you've learned. Here's a quick review of what you've learned since the last review lesson:

- **Lesson 16: Finding an implied main idea.** You practiced looking for clues in structure, language, and style, as well as the facts of the passage, to determine the main idea.
- **Lesson 17: Understanding implied causes and effects.** You learned to "read between the lines" to determine causes and make predictions about effects.
- **Lesson 18: Emotional and logical appeals.** You learned that arguments that appeal to readers' emotions need to be supported by logic as well in order to be convincing.
- **Lesson 19: Critical reading, critical thinking.** You learned different strategies to help you decide whether to accept ideas and opinions of authors or reject them.

- **Lesson 20: Finding the theme in literature.** You used your detective skills to find the main idea implied by the structure, language, style, and action in a work of literature.
- **Lesson 21: Reading across the curriculum.** You learned that part of being a critical reader in college means approaching texts from different academic disciplines in unique ways.

If any of these terms or strategies sound unfamiliar to you, STOP. Please take a few minutes to review whatever lesson is unclear.

PRACTICE

Today, you'll practice the skills listed above in combination with skills covered earlier in this book:

- Finding the facts
- Determining the main idea
- Determining the meaning of unfamiliar words
- Distinguishing between fact and opinion
- Chronological order
- Order of importance
- Cause and effect
- Comparison and contrast
- Point of view
- Diction
- Language and style
- Tone

If this seems like a monumental task, don't worry: it isn't. You've already mastered some of these skills and should be very comfortable with the others. In fact, you will probably be surprised at how easy you find this exercise to be.

PRACTICE PASSAGE

Are you ready? Read the following essay. Remember, read actively and make observations in the space provided on the next page. Then answer the questions that follow. This will give you a chance to see how well your reading skills are coming along.

Although many companies offer tuition reimbursement, most companies only reimburse employees for classes that are relevant to their position. This is a very limiting policy. A company that reimburses employees for all college credit courses—whether job related or not—offers a service not only to the employees, but to the entire company.

One good reason for giving employees unconditional tuition reimbursement is that it shows the company's dedication to its employees. In today's economy, where job security is a thing of the past and employees feel more and more expendable, it is important for a company to demonstrate to its employees that it cares. The best way to do this is with concrete investments in them.

In turn, this dedication to the betterment of company employees will create greater employee loyalty. A company that puts out funds to pay for the education of its employees will get its money back by having employees stay with the company longer. It will reduce employee turnover, because even employees who don't take advantage of the tuition reimbursement program will be more loyal to their company just knowing that their company cares enough to pay for their education.

Most importantly, the company that has an unrestricted tuition reimbursement program will have higher quality employees. Although these companies do indeed run the risk of losing money on employees who go on to another job in a different company as soon as they get their degree, more often than not, the employee will stay with the company. And even if employees do leave after graduation, it generally takes several years to complete any degree program. Thus, even if the employee leaves upon graduating, throughout those years the employer will have a more sophisticated, more intelligent, and, therefore, more valuable and productive employee. And, if the employee stays, that education will doubly benefit the company: Not only is the employee more educated, but now that employee can be promoted so the company doesn't have to fill a high-level vacancy from the outside. Open positions can be filled by people who already know the company well.

Though unconditional tuition reimbursement requires a significant investment on the employer's part, it is perhaps one of the wisest investments a company can make.

Your Observations

Record your observations about the passage in the space below.

Questions

1. According to the passage, unconditional tuition reimbursement is good for which of the following reasons?
   a. Employees get a cheaper education.
   b. Employees become more valuable.
   c. Employees can find better jobs.

2. How, according to the passage, will unconditional tuition reimbursement reduce employee turnover?
   a. by making employees more loyal
   b. by paying employees more money
   c. by promoting education

3. The first sentence of the passage, "Although many companies offer tuition reimbursement, most companies only reimburse employees for classes that are relevant to their position," is
   a. fact
   b. opinion

4. The second sentence of the passage, "This is a very limiting policy," is
   a. fact
   b. opinion

5. This passage is organized according to which of the following strategies? (Mark all that apply.)
   a. chronological order
   b. order of importance
   c. cause and effect
   d. compare and contrast

6. The point of view used in this passage is the
   a. first person point of view
   b. second person point of view
   c. third person point of view

7. The writer most likely chose this point of view because
   a. the writer is describing a personal experience
   b. it enables readers to identify with the situation
   c. its objectivity encourages the reader to take the writer's ideas seriously

8. The writer most likely uses the word *wisest* in the last sentence, rather than words such as *profitable*, *practical*, or *beneficial*, because
a. wisdom is associated with education, the subject of the essay
b. the writer trying to appeal to people who are already highly educated

9. Which of the following words best describes the tone of this essay?
a. playful
b. optimistic
c. insincere

10. The passage suggests that, compared to employees of companies that offer unconditional tuition reimbursement, employees of companies that do not offer this benefit are
a. less loyal
b. more likely to be promoted
c. not as smart

11. "Expendable" (paragraph 2) most nearly means
a. expensive
b. flexible
c. replaceable

12. The writer appeals primarily to the reader's
a. emotions
b. sense of logic

13. The main idea of the passage is that
a. companies should reimburse employees for work-related courses
b. both companies and employees would benefit from unconditional tuition reimbursement
c. companies should require their employees to take college courses

14. Which of the following would be the most credible author for this passage?
a. an employee of a company that does not offer tuition reimbursement who wants to get a bachelor's degree
b. a director of human resources for a large company who specializes in employee benefits
c. a college student majoring in accounting

Answers

1. b. The idea that employees will become more valuable if they take courses is stated in the fourth paragraph: "Thus . . . the employer will have a more sophisticated, more intelligent, and therefore more valuable and productive employee."

2. a. The idea that employees will become more loyal is stated in the third paragraph: "A company that puts out funds to pay for the education of its employees will get its money back by having employees stay with the company longer. It will reduce employee turnover because even employees who don't take advantage of the tuition reimbursement program will be more loyal. . . ."

3. a. The sentence is a fact; you could verify it by surveying companies to find out about their tuition reimbursement policies.

4. b. The sentence is an opinion; it shows how the author feels about the policy.

5. b, c. The author lists the ways companies would benefit by having unconditional tuition reimbursement in order of importance from least to most important. The author also shows the positive effects unconditional reimbursement would have on the company.

6. c. There is no *I* or *you* here; the writer doesn't refer directly to herself or to the reader. Instead, everything is spoken of in the third person.

7. c. The writer most likely uses the third person point of view because it is objective, and her argument is more likely to be taken seriously. If she used the first person, readers might think she was an employee who wanted her employer to pay for her tuition, and she wouldn't be taken seriously.

8. a. By using a word associated with education, the writer stresses the importance of education for the company.

9. b. The passage describes only positive effects of unconditional reimbursement; there is scarcely a negative word.

10. a. If employees of companies that offer unconditional tuition reimbursement are more loyal to their companies (see the second and third paragraphs), it follows that other employees will be less loyal because their company isn't showing enough dedication to their betterment.

11. c. Your best clue that *expendable* means *replaceable* is that the writer uses the word immediately after saying that job security is a thing of the past, so that workers don't feel they are important or valuable to a company that can fire them on a moment's notice.

12. b. There is common sense or reason behind each of the writer's arguments. Indeed, there are few, if any, emotional appeals in this passage.

13. b. This main idea is explicitly stated in the last sentence of the first paragraph (a good place to look for the main idea of a longer passage like this one) and repeated at the end of the passage.

14. b. The director of human resources has the most experience in this area, particularly in comparison to the college student. The employee who wants a bachelor's degree is likely to be biased in favor of tuition reimbursement for personal reasons.

How did you do? If you got all of the answers correct, congratulations! Good work. If you missed a few, you might want to take time to review the corresponding lessons.

If you missed:	Then study:
Question 1	Lesson 1
Question 2	Lesson 1
Question 3	Lesson 4
Question 4	Lesson 4
Question 5	Lessons 6–10
Question 6	Lesson 11
Question 7	Lesson 11
Question 8	Lesson 12
Question 9	Lesson 14
Question 10	Lessons 16 and 17
Question 11	Lesson 3
Question 12	Lesson 18
Question 13	Lessons 2 and 16
Question 14	Lesson 19

CONGRATULATIONS!

You've completed 22 lessons and have seen your reading skills increase. The next lesson will give you step-by-step advice on preparing for and taking exams—which you'll see plenty of during your college career. And don't forget the Appendix, which gives suggestions for how to continue to improve your reading skills, along with a list of suggested books organized by subject categories.

Now it's time to reward yourself for a job well done. Buy yourself a good book and enjoy!

L·E·S·S·O·N 23

HOW TO PREPARE FOR A TEST

LESSON SUMMARY

This lesson will show you a step-by-step process you can use to prepare for any upcoming test, whether it's an in-class essay test, a multiple-choice midterm, or a lengthy final exam. You'll find out how you can use the skills that you learned in this book to prepare for a wide variety of tests that you'll take throughout your college career. First, you'll find a time-line to help you plan a study schedule for your tests. Then, you'll learn several test strategies you can employ while actually taking a test, including how to use specific reading skills to answer typical test questions in courses ranging from history to anthropology to literature.

Many students get nervous or anxious thinking about taking an upcoming test or final exam, so don't feel you're alone if you experience such feelings. The best way to combat test anxiety is to **be prepared**. You've probably heard that advice before but may not know exactly how to go about it.

This lesson will show you several ways to prepare for upcoming tests. The fact that you're reading this book gives you a distinct advantage because you've already increased your reading skills by completing the lessons in this book. And increased reading skills, along with a solid study plan, will help you improve your test scores.

An important step in preparing for your tests is to be aware of when they will occur. With the hectic pace of college life, it can be easy to forget a test date. Therefore, it's best to write down all upcoming test dates on your calendar. That way, you won't be caught off guard. Once you've charted all your test dates in a calendar, you can set up a plan of preparation.

PREPARING FOR YOUR TEST STEP-BY-STEP

Several test preparation timelines are presented below. You can write each stage down on your calendar. These steps will work well for midterm and final exams, as well as for any other tests your instructor gives you at least three weeks' notice for. Of course, if you have an instructor who gives pop quizzes unannounced, then you need to be ready every day you have class. However, you usually will have at least three or four weeks' notice for upcoming exams. Indeed, most instructors will give you a *syllabus*, or course outline, at the beginning of the course with all the test dates clearly marked. Follow the steps below to confidently face your next test.

THREE OR FOUR WEEKS BEFORE THE TEST

Plan ahead. About a month before the test, take the following steps:

1. Ask your instructor to clarify what will be on the test. Take notes on whatever the instructor tells you and focus your review on those items that will be tested.

2. Review your notes from class lectures. Get copies of any notes you missed from other students or the instructor. Read your lecture notes using the reading tools discussed in this book to get the most out of them.

3. Review all assigned textbook readings, paying special attention to any marginal notes or highlighting you did. Now that you know how to find main ideas in a written work, it's time to use that knowledge. Write down each chapter's main idea in the margin of the book or in your class notebook for later review.

4. Create flash cards to memorize key concepts, dates, or terms that you think will be on the test. Carry the flash cards with you so you can pull them out and study them whenever you have a few minutes of downtime. Before you create a flash card for an unfamiliar term in your assigned reading, try to determine the word's meaning from its context in the textbook before looking it up in a dictionary.

TWO WEEKS BEFORE THE TEST

Now is the time to get some more specific information about your test, so follow these guidelines:

1. Ask your instructor how the test will be organized— true/false, multiple choice, essay, fill-in-the-blank, short answer, essay, and so on.

2. Find out how much the test will affect your grade. If it's a final exam worth 50 percent of your grade, you'll want to spend more time studying than for a weekly test worth 5 percent of your grade. Check with your instructor or look at the syllabus you received at the beginning of the term.

3. Pretend you're the instructor—what would you ask on this test? Make up a few sample questions and then write out your answers to them. You just might find those same questions on the test!

4. Jot down any questions you have about the material you're reviewing to ask the instructor. It's better to clarify your questions before the test than after.

ONE WEEK BEFORE THE TEST

During the week before the test, you should be intensifying your study so you won't have to cram the day before the exam.

1. Review your notes again and highlight the portions that you don't know yet. Then the next time you review, you won't have to re-read all the information that you already know; instead, you can focus on learning or memorizing the highlighted information.

2. Continue studying your flash cards of important terms, dates, and facts. Create more flash cards as needed.

3. Create lists, outlines, rhymes, or anything else that will help you remember the information you are studying.

4. Study with another student or group of students. A small group works better than a large one. Stay focused on the material and discuss concepts and possible test questions with each other.

TWO OR THREE DAYS BEFORE THE TEST

In the few days before the test, take care of your body as well as of your mind.

1. Continue your review. Since you started reviewing early, there is no need to cram at this point. Cramming may confuse you and take away your body's energy—and you'll need that energy on test day!

2. Do some physical activity to increase the oxygen flow to your brain. Don't wear yourself out trying to run a marathon, but moderate exercise will help your brain to achieve peak performance during the upcoming test. Brisk walking is an excellent energy-building exercise.

3. Eat a well-balanced diet so you won't get fatigued or become sick before you take the test. You'll want to be in good health so your brain will function clearly during the test. Don't fall prey to the cramming, coffee-drinking, no-sleep lifestyle that has become popular among some students right before test time. It's just not worth the damage to your health, and it could prevent you from doing well on the test.

4. Along with exercise and eating right, it's important to get enough sleep before the big day. You don't want to fall asleep while you're in the middle of writing a great answer to an essay question only to find that you don't have time to finish it once you awaken.

THE DAY OF THE TEST

Here are some tips to help you do well on test day:

1. Allow extra time to get to class or the examining room early, so you don't have to rush. If you miss an important announcement at the beginning of class, it could hurt your score.

2. Ensure that you have all the materials you need. If you are allowed to bring a textbook, dictionary, or other reference, by all means do so. You may need scratch paper to write on during the test. Bring extra pens or pencils too.

3. Listen carefully to all of the announcements and directions given by the instructor before you begin. Even if the test is in front of you,

don't become so distracted by it that you don't hear what the instructor is saying. Sometimes instructors override what is written on the test itself or will tell you to write in a change.

4. Look quickly through the entire test to see how many questions are asked. Be sure you know how much time you have, and read all written instructions carefully. Take a moment to jot down an estimate of how much time you can spend on each portion or question. If three essay questions are asked and you have 60 minutes to complete the test, then you can spend 20 minutes on each one.

STRATEGIES TO USE DURING THE TEST

Once you've read the directions carefully, looked briefly over the entire test, and mentally noted the amount of time you have, you can begin working with confidence. Here are several strategies that you can use while you are actually taking the test to increase your chances of getting a good score. They include managing emotional issues, using your time wisely, avoiding errors, using your reading skills to answer tough questions, knowing tips on how to get the right answers, and checking your work if you finish early.

MANAGING EMOTIONAL ISSUES
Take the Test One Question at a Time
Focus all of your attention on the one question you're answering. Block out any thoughts about questions you've already finished or concerns about what's coming next. Concentrate your thinking where it will do the most good—on the question you're answering now.

Develop a Positive Attitude
Keep reminding yourself that you're prepared. In fact, if you've completed the lessons in this book, you're probably better prepared than many others who are taking the test. Remember, it's only a test, and you're going to do your **best**. That's all anyone can ask of you. If that nagging drill sergeant voice inside your head starts sending negative messages, combat them with positive ones of your own. Tell yourself:

- "I'm doing just fine."
- "I've prepared for this test."
- "I know exactly what to do."
- "I know I can get the score I'm shooting for."

You get the idea. Remember to drown out negative messages with positive ones of your own.

If You Lose Your Concentration
Don't worry about it! It's normal. During a long test it happens to everyone. When your mind is stressed or overexerted, it takes a break whether you want it to or not. It's easy to get your concentration back if you simply acknowledge the fact that you've lost it and take a quick break. You brain needs very little time (seconds, really) to rest.

Put your pencil down and close your eyes. Take a deep breath, hold it for a moment, and let it out slowly. Listen to the sound of your breathing as you repeat this two more times. The few seconds that this takes is really all the time your brain needs to relax and get ready to focus again. This exercise also helps you control your heart rate so you can keep anxiety at bay.

Try this technique several times in the days before the test when you feel stressed. The more you practice, the better it will work for you on the day of the test.

If You Freeze

Don't worry about a question that stumps you even though you're sure you know the answer. Mark it and go on to the next question. You can come back to the "stumper" later. Try to put it out of your mind completely until you come back to it. Just let your subconscious mind chew on the question while your conscious mind focuses on the other questions (one at a time—of course). Chances are, the memory block will be gone by the time you return to the question.

If you freeze before you even begin the test, here's what to do:

1. Do some deep breathing to help yourself relax and focus.

2. Remind yourself that you're prepared.

3. Take a little time to look over the test.

4. Read a few of the questions.

5. Decide which ones are the easiest and start there.

Before long, you'll be "in the groove."

TIME STRATEGIES

One of the most important—and nerve-wracking—elements of taking a test is time. You'll only be allowed a certain amount of time to complete the test, so it's important to use every minute wisely.

Pace Yourself

The most important time strategy is **pacing yourself.** Before you begin, take just a few seconds to survey the test, making note of the number of questions and of the sections that look easier than the rest. Then, make a rough time schedule based on the amount of time available to you. Mark the halfway point on your test and make a note beside that mark of what the time will be when the testing period is half over.

Keep Moving

Once you begin the test, **keep moving.** If you work slowly in an attempt to make fewer mistakes, your mind will become bored and begin to wander. You'll end up making far more mistakes if you're not concentrating. Worse, if you take too long to answer questions that stump you, you may end up running out of time before you finish.

So don't stop for difficult questions. Skip them and move on. You can come back to them later if you have time. Answering the easier questions first helps to build your confidence and gets you in the testing groove. Who knows? As you go through the test, you may even stumble across some relevant information to help you answer those tough questions.

Don't Rush

Keep moving, but **don't rush.** Think of your mind as a seesaw. On one side is your emotional energy. On the other side is your intellectual energy. When your emotional energy is high, your intellectual capacity is low. Remember how difficult it is to reason with someone when you're angry? On the other hand, when your intellectual energy is high, your emotional energy is low. Rushing raises your emotional energy and reduces your intellectual capacity. Move quickly to keep your mind from wandering, but don't rush and get yourself flustered.

Check Yourself

Check yourself at the halfway mark. If you're a little ahead, you know you're on track and may even have a little time left to check your work. If you're a little behind, you have several choices. You can pick up the pace a little, but do this *only* if you can do it comfortably. Remember—**don't rush!** You can also skip around in the remaining portion of the test to pick up as many easy points as possible. This strategy has one drawback, however. If you are marking a bubble-style answer sheet, and you put the right answers in the wrong bubbles—they're wrong. So pay close attention to the question numbers if you decide to do this.

AVOIDING ERRORS

When you take the test, you want to make as few errors as possible in the questions you answer. Here are a few tactics to keep in mind.

Control Yourself

Remember that comparison between your mind and a seesaw? Keeping your emotional energy low and your intellectual energy high is the best way to avoid mistakes. If you feel stressed or worried, stop for a few seconds. Acknowledge the feeling (Hmmm! I'm feeling a little pressure here!), take a few deep breaths, and send yourself a few positive messages. This relieves your emotional anxiety and boosts your intellectual capacity.

Mark Answers Carefully

This may seem like a silly warning, but it is important. Place your answers in the right blanks or the corresponding ovals on the answer sheet if your instructor uses an electronically scored test. Right answers in the wrong place earn no points. It's a good idea to check every five to ten questions to make sure you're in the right spot. That way you won't need much time to correct your answer sheet if you have made an error.

If you are writing your answers on the test itself or a separate sheet of paper, be sure to write neatly and clearly. You could get points taken off if the instructor can't read your handwriting.

USING SPECIFIC READING SKILLS

Your increased reading skills will enable you to perform better on a wide variety of tests. Here are some practical examples of the types of test questions you can

expect from beginning college courses and the specific reading skills you can use to master them.

Is It Fact or Opinion?

Now that you know the difference between what an author knows to be true and what an author believes to be true, you can use this knowledge to answer several kinds of true/false test questions. For instance, if you're taking a test in an American history course, you may find a true/false statement such as "The Civil War should have been won by the South." After studying the difference between fact and opinion, you can clearly see that this is an opinion and not a fact. However, the statement "The Civil War was won by the North" is a verifiable fact and not an opinion, so you would mark it as true. Of course, you must know your history facts for this tip to work.

Order of Importance and Compare/Contrast

If you're asked to analyze an article written by a prominent anthropologist for an in-class essay test in a social science course, you'll know that you can look for the order of ideas that the author presents to see what is most important to her. Then you'll know which points you should spend more time discussing in your answer. Another reading skill you've practiced in this book is how to identify an author's use of comparison and contrast. Therefore, you'll be able to tell if the author used this method of organization in the article. If so, you'll know how to find her main idea.

Cause and Effect

When you practiced identifying causes and effects in a piece of writing in an earlier lesson, you gave yourself a big advantage in taking tests that require this type of analysis. For example, students are often asked to list the causes or effects of various wars in a world history course. Now that you've studied how to tell the difference between causes and effects and how to identify them in the material you read, this type of question shouldn't give you any trouble.

Reading Between the Lines

If you're taking a basic course on the American government and its political parties, you may be given a test that asks you to read between the lines of a written campaign speech or a political candidate's statement of purpose. You'll be able to examine the author's tone, style, structure, and use of emotional and logical appeals and determine if there are any hidden agendas or implied ideas within the work. This information will not only help you answer questions on a test, but it will also help you to become a more informed voter.

Identifying Themes

You'll often be asked to find and discuss the theme of a written work in a college course. For instance, in an introduction to literature course, students may have to identify and discuss the themes present in a novel by Jane Austen or a poem by William Shakespeare for an in-class essay test. Since you practiced the skill of identifying themes in literature in this book, you'll be prepared for this type of question. In fact, you should be able to discuss how action and language in a written work are added together to achieve the work's theme.

Reading Comprehension Passages

You may encounter a test that contains reading comprehension passages with a series of questions that follow them. Use the following tips to ace these types of test questions.

This may seem strange, but sometimes a few questions can be answered without reading the passage. If the passage is short, a paragraph with four sentences or so, read the questions first. After you've read the questions, you'll know what to look for while reading the passage. This focuses your reading and makes it easier for you to retain important information.

If a reading passage is long and is followed by more than ten questions, it will take some time to read the questions first. Even so, take a minute or two to skim the questions and read a few of the shorter ones. Then, read the passage actively by marking it up while you read. If you find a sentence that seems to state the main idea of the passage, underline it. As you read the rest of the passage, number the main points that support the main idea. Several questions will deal with this information. If it's underlined and numbered, you can locate it easily. Other questions will ask for specific details. **Circle** information that tells who, what, when, or where. The circles will be easy to locate later if you run across a question that asks for specific information. Marking up a passage in this way also heightens your concentration and makes it more likely that you'll remember the information when you answer the questions following the passage.

GETTING THE RIGHT ANSWERS

Make sure you understand what the question is asking before you answer it. If you're not sure of what's being asked, you won't know whether you're giving the right answer. You can use the tips given below to help you select the right answers for multiple-choice, true/false, fill-in-the-blank, and essay questions. Since these questions are so different from each other, helpful hints for getting the right answers are given for each type.

Multiple-Choice Questions

For multiple-choice questions, if the answer isn't readily apparent, look for clues in the answer choices. Notice the similarities and differences in the answer choices. Sometimes this helps to put the question in a new perspective and makes it easier to answer. If you're still not sure of the answer, use the process of elimination. First, eliminate any answer choices that are obviously wrong. Then reason your way through the remaining choices. You may be able to use relevant information from other parts of the test. If you can't eliminate any of the answer choices, you might be better off to skip the question and come back to it later. If you can't eliminate any answer choices to improve your odds when you come back later, just make a guess and move on.

True/False Questions

If the question is true/false style, read the entire statement before deciding if it's true or false. For a statement to be true, the entire statement must be true. Often, the first part of a statement will be true, but the second part will be false. Use the reading skill of distinguishing between fact and opinion for help in answering these questions. Look for words that signal extremes, such as *never, always, everyone, all,* or *none.* Statements with these words in them are often false just because they include these extreme words.

Fill-in-the-Blank Questions

If the question is a fill-in-the-blank one, remember to look closely at the question for clues to the answer. For example, is the word before the blank *a* or *an?* If so, you'll know whether the word you need to fill in the blank should begin with a vowel or a consonant.

You can also look at the length of the blank line since it might tell you if the answer you are to write in is long or short. As long as your instructor doesn't take points away for guessing, you might as well take your best guess on these questions. Think back to the flash cards you made or the lists of terms specific to the test's subject and insert one of those words that seem applicable.

Essay Questions

If you're answering an essay question, it's very important to read and re-read the question very carefully before you plunge into answering it. If you misread what the question is asking, you could waste valuable time and points by answering the wrong question. Practice being an active reader by using the reading skills covered in this book to fully understand what the question is asking.

Several key words are often used in essay questions, so you'll have a head start if you know what they mean before the test. If you are unsure of the meaning of any of the following words, look those words up in a dictionary and memorize their meanings before taking an essay test.

compare	describe	list
contrast	discuss	outline
criticize	evaluate	prove
define	interpret	review

After you read the question very carefully and know what it is asking, jot down an outline or at least a list of items you plan to include in your answer before you begin writing. Taking a few minutes to organize your answer before you begin can increase your score dramatically and can also eliminate the need for scribbling out sentences and trying to squeeze in extra facts you forgot the first time. Spend more time creating strong topic sentences for each paragraph than randomly writing down all the details you can remember about the topic. Using these tips will help you to perform better on the next essay test you encounter.

IF YOU FINISH EARLY

Use any time you have left at the end of the test to check your work. First, make certain you've put the answers in the right places, especially if you're marking a bubble-style answer sheet. Also, make sure you've answered each question only once. Questions with more than one answer are usually marked wrong. If you've erased an answer, make sure you've done a good job. Check for stray marks on your answer sheet that could distort your score.

After you've checked for these easy errors, take a second look at the more difficult questions. You've probably heard the folk wisdom about never changing an answer. It's not always good advice. If you have a good reason for thinking a response is wrong, change it.

If you're taking an essay test, look back over your answers and take the time to correct any spelling errors or to add words you may have forgotten to write in the first time. It's easy to miss writing the words *the* or *an* when you're writing quickly. If you need to make a small correction, neatly cross out the word and carefully write your correction above it. Instructors don't like to read messy essay answers that are full of cross-outs and scribbles, so be as neat as you can when changing or adding words to your answer.

AFTER THE TEST

Once you've finished, *congratulate yourself*. You've worked hard to prepare; now it's time to enjoy yourself and relax. Plan a celebration or treat yourself to a fancy dinner or a new sweater. You deserve it after all your hard work.

Skill Building One Last Time

Choose one upcoming test that you have to study for and write down a study plan for it using the timeline given in this lesson. Jot down specific steps you'll take to prepare for the test, such as re-reading chapters 2–6 in the assigned textbook, asking the instructor to review the principles listed in chapter 4 that you weren't sure of, or reviewing one or more of the lessons in this book. After you complete this exercise, carry the study plan with you, so you can remember to complete each step as your test date draws near.

A·P·P·E·N·D·I·X
ADDITIONAL RESOURCES

Reading is like exercise: If you don't keep doing it, you'll get out of shape. Like muscles that grow stronger and bigger with each repetition, your reading skills will grow stronger and stronger with each text that you read. But if you stop working out, your reading comprehension muscles will deteriorate, and you may find yourself struggling with material that you could have easily understood several months ago.

So don't stop now! You've really just begun. Reading comprehension is a skill to build throughout your whole lifetime.

TIPS FOR CONTINUING TO IMPROVE YOUR READING

The following are some ways you can continue to strengthen your reading comprehension skills:

- **Read!** Read anything—books, newspapers, magazines, novels, poems. The more you read, the better. Set yourself a reading goal: one book a month, two books while you're on vacation, a half hour of reading every night before bed. There's a list of suggested books at the end of this section; try some.
- **Discover new authors.** Check out the best-seller list and try one of the books on that list. If it's a best-seller, it's probably a book that appeals to a wide variety of readers, and chances are good that you'll like it.

- **Spend time in bookstores and libraries.** There are bound to be books and authors out there that appeal to some of your interests. Don't be afraid to ask a salesperson or librarian to help you: Describe your interests and your preferences in style, and he or she can help you find books you'll enjoy reading.
- **Join a reading group.** Most cities and towns have a club that meets every two weeks or each month to discuss a selected book. In these groups, you'll get to discuss your ideas and questions with a group of friends and associates in an informal setting. If your area doesn't have a reading group, start your own. You and your friends can take turns choosing which book you'll read and discuss.
- **Review this book periodically to refresh yourself about the basics.** Try some of the Skill Building exercises at the end of each lesson on a regular basis.

SUGGESTED READING LIST

Below is a list of books, organized by subject categories. Choose a category that interests you, and try some of the books listed there.

Science Fiction

Fahrenheit 451 by Ray Bradbury
The Left Hand of Darkness by Ursula LeGuin
Stranger in a Strange Land by Robert Heinlein
1984 by George Orwell
Jurassic Park by Michael Crighton

Science/Medicine

The Lives of a Cell by Lewis Thomas
Mortal Lessons by Richard Selzer

Fantasy

The Hobbit by J. R. R. Tolkien
On a Pale Horse by Piers Anthony

Autobiography

The Autobiography of Malcolm X by Malcolm X
The Story of My Life by Helen Keller
The Diary of Anne Frank by Anne Frank
The Heroic Slave by Frederick Douglas
I Know Why the Caged Bird Sings by Maya Angelou
Having Our Say by Sarah L. and Elizabeth Delaney
Black Boy by Richard Wright
Everything I Need to Know I Learned in Kindergarten by Robert Fulghum

Historical/Social Issues

Of Mice and Men by John Steinbeck
The Color Purple by Alice Walker
The Last of the Mohicans by James Fenimore Cooper
To Kill a Mockingbird by Harper Lee
The Joy Luck Club by Amy Tan
The Sun Also Rises by Ernest Hemingway
The Lord of the Flies by William Golding
Dangerous Minds by LouAnne Johnson
Schindler's List by Thomas Keneally

War

Red Badge of Courage by Stephen Crane
All Quiet on the Western Front by Erich Maria Remarque
Hiroshima by John Hershey

Coming of Age

A Separate Peace by John Knowles

The Catcher in the Rye by J. D. Salinger

The House on Mango Street by Sandra Cisneros

Short Stories

The short stories of Ernest Hemingway

Love Life by Bobbie Ann Mason

Girls at War by Chinua Achebe

The Stories of Eva Luna by Isabel Allende

Inspirational/Spiritual

A Simple Path by Mother Theresa

The Tibetan Book of Living and Dying
     by Sogyal Rinpoche

Care of the Soul by Thomas Moore

Hinds' Feet on High Places by Hannah Hurnard

The Tao of Pooh and *The Te of Piglet*
     by Benjamin Hoff

The Holy Bible

The Koran

Tao Te Ching by Lao Tzu

Detective/Thriller

Agatha Christie's murder mysteries

A Time To Kill, The Client by John Grisham

The "A is for . . . " series by Sue Grafton

Novels by Sara Paretsky

Sherlock Holmes stories by Sir Arthur Conan Doyle

Mythology

Mythology by Edith Hamilton

American Indian Myths and Legends by Richard Erdoes and Alfonso Ortiz